TOP TIPS FOR THE TOEIC® L&R TEST

TOEIC is a registered trademark of Educational Testing Service (ETS). This publication is not endorsed or approved by ETS.
*L&R means Listening and Reading.

Shari J. Berman   Hiroko Kobayashi   Makoto Hayasaka

考えて解くTOEIC® L&R TEST実践演習

音声ファイルのダウンロード／ストリーミング

CD マーク表示がある箇所は、音声を弊社 HP より無料でダウンロード／ストリーミングすることができます。トップページのバナーをクリックし、書籍検索してください。書籍詳細ページに音声ダウンロードアイコンがございますのでそちらから自習用音声としてご活用ください。

https://www.seibido.co.jp

TOP TIPS FOR THE TOEIC® L&R TEST

はしがき

　本テキストは、学生たちが通年の授業の中で、**THE TOEIC® L&R TEST** におけるスコア 550 点前後の獲得を共通の目標として、総合的な英語力を確実に身につけることができるよう書き下ろした 2 部構成の教材です。

本書の特長

1 前半はパート別、後半はトピック別の 2 部構成

これが本テキストの最大の特長です。第 1 部の Unit 1 から 6 は、パート別（Part 1 から Part 7）の構成、第 2 部の Unit 7 から 14 はトピック別に全パートを学習する全パート横断型の構成です。

2 考えて解く実践演習

学生が自分で考えながら問題を解き、無理なく実践力を獲得できるよう構成しました。第 1 部ではパート別に、まず戦略と分析を行い、何に留意しどう考えて問題に取り組むかを把握したうえで設問を解き、第 2 部では、学生が興味を持つトピックごとに、リスニング・リーディングセクションの間違えやすいポイントに沿って設問を解きます。

3 どのレベルの学習者にも対応

THE TOEIC® L&R TEST がどのレベルの学習者でも受験できるのと同様に、本テキストも学生はどのレベルからでも利用できます。このことが可能なのは、学生が苦手とする語彙や文法という基礎的課題の再確認や、ナチュラルスピードのリスニングスクリプトも段階を追って繰り返し聞くことで、無理なく聞きこなせる演習を取り入れているからです。

4 各章に TOEIC 模擬問題

第 1 部、第 2 部とも Mini Practice Test（TOEIC 模擬問題）を掲載しました。いずれもその章で学習したことに関連のある模擬問題となっています。

　本テキストの、全編を通じた『TOP TIPS（最高に有益なヒント）』が、学生の皆さんの目標達成の一助となれば幸いです。

　最後になりましたが、本テキストの作成にあたっては株式会社成美堂の編集部の方々に多大な労を執っていただきました。ここに感謝の意を表します。

著　者

各 Unit の構成

●第1部　パート別

	パート名	Step 1	Step 2	Step 3	Mini Practice Test（模擬問題）セット数
Listening Section					
Unit 1	Part 1	Overview（概観）	Strategy（戦略）	Analysis（分析）	4
	Part 2	Overview（概観）	Strategy（戦略）	Analysis（分析）	5
Unit 2	Part3	Overview（概観）	Strategy（戦略）	Analysis（分析）	4
					2人の会話、3人の会話
					図表、発言の意図
Unit 3	Part 4	Overview（概観）	Strategy（戦略）	Analysis（分析）	3
					図表・発言の意図なし
					図表、発言の意図

	パート名	Step 1	Step 2	Step 3	Mini Practice Test（模擬問題）セット数
Reading Section					
Unit 4	Part 5	Overview（概観）	Strategy（戦略）	Analysis（分析）	10
Unit 5	Part 6	Overview（概観）	Strategy（戦略）	Analysis（分析）	3
Unit 6	Part 7	Overview（概観）	Strategy（戦略）	Analysis（分析）	3
					テキストメッセージ
					シングル、ダブル

●第2部（トピック別）

リスニングセクションの構成
1. Sound Advice 2. Vocabulary Warm-up 3. Mini Practice Test (模擬問題)

	トピック	課題	Part 1	Part 2	Part 3	Part 4
Listening Section			Mini Practice Test（模擬問題）セット数			
Unit 7	交通	リエゾン	2	4	1	1
					発言の意図	図表
Unit 8	メニュー・旅行日程	最初の語	2	4	1	1
					発言の意図	図表
Unit 9	販売・注文	カタカナ英語	2	4	1	1
					3人の会話	
Unit 10	余暇	can と can't	2	4	1	1
						図表
Unit 11	放送	ストレス（強調）	2	4	1	1
						図表
Unit 12	議題	How の疑問文	2	4	1	1
						発言の意図
Unit 13	オフィス	同音異義語	2	4	1	1
					発言の意図	
Unit 14	面接	状況のイメージ	2	4	1	1
						図表

リーディングセクションの構成
1. Grammar Review 2. Mini Practice Test（模擬問題）

			Reading Section		
			Mini Practice Test（模擬問題）セット数		
	トピック	課題	Part 5	Part 6	Part 7
Unit 7	交通	形容詞	3	1	1
		-ed と -ing			テキストメッセージ（2問）
Unit 8	メニュー・旅行日程	前置詞	3	1	1
					トリプル（5問）
Unit 9	販売・注文	副詞	3	1	1
		almost, almost all, most			シングル（3問）
Unit 10	余暇	不定詞と動名詞	3	1	1
					トリプル（5問）
Unit 11	放送	接続詞と前置詞	3	1	1
					トリプル（5問）
Unit 12	議題	頻度を表す副詞	3	1	1
					テキストメッセージ（3問）
Unit 13	オフィス	現在完了	3	1	1
					ダブル（5問）
Unit 14	面接	仮定法過去・過去完了	3	1	1
					ダブル（5問）

目　　次

第1部　パート別

第2部　トピック別

PARTS

第1部
パート別

- **Unit 1 Part 1 & Part 2**（写真描写問題・応答問題）
- **Unit 2 Part 3**（会話問題）
- **Unit 3 Part 4**（説明文問題）
- **Unit 4 Part 5**（短文穴埋め問題）
- **Unit 5 Part 6**（長文穴埋め問題）
- **Unit 6 Part 7**（読解問題）

Part 1 & Part 2

Part 1 写真描写問題 (Photographs)

Step 1 | Overview (概観)

◆ **Format** (構成)

Part 1 写真描写問題は、放送される4つの説明文 (statements) の中から、写真を見て最も的確に描写しているものを選ぶ問題で、全6問です。4つの短い説明文は1度放送されるだけで、印刷されていません。

出題例

Ⓐ Ⓑ Ⓒ Ⓓ

Step 2 | Strategy (戦略)

◆ **PREVIEW** (準備)　解答用紙を開いたら…

> 説明文が聞こえてくる前に、写真を見て素早く頭の中でどのような物や人が見えるかを考えましょう。(=quick mental note)

What can you see clearly here?

Q: 写真の中で、「はっきりと」見えるものを以下の中から選んで☑してください。

1 buses ☐	**2** buildings ☐	**3** cars ☐	**4** clouds ☐	**5** dogs ☐
6 gates ☐	**7** parking spaces ☐	**8** people ☐	**9** trees ☐	**10** umbrellas ☐

前ページの写真について設問の応答として最も適切なものを1つ選んでください。実際のテストでは説明文は印刷されていませんが、ここでは音声と共に以下の説明文を読んで適切なものを選んでください。

(A) A woman is getting into her car.

(B) Many people are standing outside the building.

(C) A car is turning into the parking lot.

(D) There are several cars in the parking lot.

Ⓐ Ⓑ Ⓒ Ⓓ

Step3 | Analysis（分析）

🌑 Analysis **1** 説明文のパターンは2つ

説明文は、カメラが捉えた①何かの動き「verb-based 行動（＝動詞主導型)」あるいは、②人や物の「state 状況」を描写しています。

① **V**「verb-based 行動＝動詞主導型」
このパターンの説明文は主に、現在進行形 つまり"-ing" をとります。
- X is doing Y
  例) He's placing a bag into the overhead compartment.

② **S**「state 状況」
このパターンの説明文は主に以下のいずれかの文型をとります。
- There is a/an X [on/ in/ next/ in front of/ behind] the Y.
  例) There is a big tree in front of the building.

- There are [some/ several/ many] Xs [on/ in/ near/ next to/ in front of/ behind] the Y.
  例) There are lots of passengers on the train.

- The X [is made/ consists] of Y.
  例) This house is made of candy.

- The X is [open/ closed/ out of order].
  例) This vending machine is out of order.

● **Exercise** **1**   1-04〜08

写真について5つの説明文を聞き、V (verb-based 行動) または S (state 状況) のどちらを
示すかを判断して☑してください。

(1) V ☐ S ☐	(4) V ☐ S ☐
(2) V ☐ S ☐	(5) V ☐ S ☐
(3) V ☐ S ☐	

● **Exercise** **2**   1-09

では、同じ写真を使って模擬問題を解いてみましょう。4つの説明文を聞き、最も適切なもの
を1つ選んでください。

Ⓐ Ⓑ Ⓒ Ⓓ

● **Exercise** **3**   1-10、11

写真について4つの説明文を聞き、最も適切なものを1つ選んでください。

1.   **2.**

Ⓐ Ⓑ Ⓒ Ⓓ

Ⓐ Ⓑ Ⓒ Ⓓ

◐ Analysis 2　はっきり判断できる行動・状況しか正解にならない

テストで使用する写真は白黒なので、非常に細かな描写に照準を当てた選択肢が正解となることはありません。

● Exercise 1

 1-12～16

以下の写真について5つの説明文を聞き、T（正解）かF（不正解）のどちらを示すかを判断し、☑を入れてください。

```
(1) T☐ F☐        (4) T☐ F☐

(2) T☐ F☐        (5) T☐ F☐

(3) T☐ F☐
```

● Exercise 2

 1-17、18

写真について4つの説明文を聞き、最も適切なものを1つ選んでください。

1.

Ⓐ Ⓑ Ⓒ Ⓓ

2.

Ⓐ Ⓑ Ⓒ Ⓓ

Part 2 応答問題（Question-Response）

Step1 | Overview（概観）

◆ **Format（構成）**

Part 2 応答問題では、1 つの質問または発言とそれに対する 3 つの答えがそれぞれ 1 度だけ放送されます。質問に対して最もふさわしい応答を選ぶ問題で、全 25 問です。質問も応答も印刷されていません。

出題例

Mark your answer.　　　Ⓐ　Ⓑ　Ⓒ

● **Exercise**　　　　　　　　　　　　　　　　　　　　　🎧 1-19

実際のテストでは質問も応答も印刷されていませんが、ここでは音声とともに以下の質問と応答を読んで最も適切なものを 1 つ選んでください。

Is your assistant out on vacation?

(A) Yes, I had a very good time.

(B) No, he's at a sales conference this week.

(C) I can recommend a good place.　　　Mark your answer.　　Ⓐ　Ⓑ　Ⓒ

Step2 | Strategy（戦略）

英語による質問の聞き取りでは文の前半に集中することが必要で、後半はいくらかリラックス

> 英語は、質問も応答も、冒頭に神経を集中して聞き取る。

できます。次の Wake Up! は、質問の最初の単語を集中して聞き取るエクササイズです。

⌐Wake Up!　　　　　　　　　　　　　　　　🎧 1-20〜29

これから聞く質問の最初の<u>単語</u>を聞き、以下に記入してください。
質問は、書かれている英文とは違って聞こえるかもしれません。
　例）What did you say? は Whaddya say? と聞こえますが、この場合、"What" と記載します。

(1) _____　(2) _____　(3) _____　(4) _____　(5) _____

(6) _____　(7) _____　(8) _____　(9) _____　(10) _____

Step3　Analysis（分析）

Part 2では少ない情報から状況を的確に判断し、発話のニュアンスや論理を捉える能力が試されます。

◔ Analysis 1　応答を推測できる場合

1. Why で始まる質問に対する Because のように、正解が的確に予測できる場合があります。
   例）質問　**Why** did you choose that one?
   　　応答　**Because** I thought it was perfect for my mom's present.

2. Where で始まる質問であれば、通常「場所」と関わりがあります。
   例）質問　**Where** are you going?
   　　応答　I'm going **to the store**.

3. Yes/No の返事が求められる質問であれば、agreement（同意）または disagreement（非同意）を示す単語を聞き取ればそれが正解です。
   例）質問　**Do you think** he's the one who knows the truth?
   　　応答　**No, I don't think so.**

4. "lack of knowledge"（知識不足）を表現する場合もあります。
   例）質問　Is there any post office near here?
   　　応答　Sorry, **I'm a stranger** here.

● Exercise 1
🔵 1-30、31

では分析をもとに、問題を解いてみましょう。実際のテストでは質問も応答も印刷されていませんが、ここでは質問文を表示してあります。

1. Shall we discuss it with an ad agency?　　Mark your answer.　　Ⓐ Ⓑ Ⓒ
2. What time is your flight tomorrow?　　Mark your answer.　　Ⓐ Ⓑ Ⓒ

● Exercise 2
🔵 1-32、33

設問の応答として最も適切なものを1つ選んでください。

1. Mark your answer.　　Ⓐ Ⓑ Ⓒ
2. Mark your answer.　　Ⓐ Ⓑ Ⓒ

◔ Analysis 2　Think outside the box（既存の考えにとらわれずに考える場合）

一方で既存の考えにとらわれない、ひねりの効いた応答への対応も必要です。
　例）質問　**How much is this book?**
　　　応答として正しい選択肢は次のどれですか。

(A) It's an adventure story.
(B) We only take cash.
(C) It should say on the cover.　　Mark your answer.　　Ⓐ Ⓑ Ⓒ

● **Exercise 1**　 1-34、35

では分析をもとに、問題を解いてみましょう。実際のテストでは質問も応答も印刷されていま
せんが、ここでは質問文を表示してあります。

1. Who's going on the trip tomorrow?　　Mark your answer.　　Ⓐ Ⓑ Ⓒ
2. Do you have a strategy for your speech?　Mark your answer.　Ⓐ Ⓑ Ⓒ

● **Exercise 2**　 1-36、37

設問の応答として最も適切なものを1つ選んでください。

1. Mark your answer.　　Ⓐ Ⓑ Ⓒ
2. Mark your answer.　　Ⓐ Ⓑ Ⓒ

◖ **Analysis 3**　ある程度 "read the room" (空気を読む) ことも必要

1. 最初の発話者が、質問ではなく、発言をとる場合もあります。
　例） 質問　I don't know what to order here.
　　　応答　The fresh fish is always good here.

2. 最初の発話者が、Isn't it? Wasn't it? Doesn't it? Don't you? Didn't you? などの
　tag question（付加疑問）を用いて、同意・非同意を求める場合もあります。
　例） 質問　You like mystery novels, **don't you?**
　　　応答　**Yes,** I read them all the time.

● **Exercise 1**　 1-38、39

では分析をもとに、問題を解いてみましょう。実際のテストでは質問も応答も印刷されていま
せんが、ここでは質問文を表示してあります。

1. It looks like rain, doesn't it?　　Mark your answer.　　Ⓐ Ⓑ Ⓒ
2. We're running out of paper.　　Mark your answer.　　Ⓐ Ⓑ Ⓒ

● **Exercise 2**　 1-40、41

音声を聞き、設問の応答として最も適切なものを1つ選んでください。

1. Mark your answer.　Ⓐ Ⓑ Ⓒ　　**2.** Mark your answer.　Ⓐ Ⓑ Ⓒ

▶Mini Practice Test

◆ Part 1 （写真描写問題）

CD 1-42〜45

写真について4つの説明文を聞き、最も適切なものを1つ選んでください。

1.

Ⓐ Ⓑ Ⓒ Ⓓ

2.

Ⓐ Ⓑ Ⓒ Ⓓ

3.

Ⓐ Ⓑ Ⓒ Ⓓ

4.

Ⓐ Ⓑ Ⓒ Ⓓ

◆ Part 2 （応答問題）

CD 1-46〜50

質問の応答として最も適切なものを1つ選んでください。

1. Mark your answer. Ⓐ Ⓑ Ⓒ

2. Mark your answer. Ⓐ Ⓑ Ⓒ

3. Mark your answer. Ⓐ Ⓑ Ⓒ

4. Mark your answer. Ⓐ Ⓑ Ⓒ

5. Mark your answer. Ⓐ Ⓑ Ⓒ

Unit 2

Part 3

Part 3 会話問題（Conversations）

Step 1 Overview（概観）

◆ Format（構成）

・2人あるいは3人による会話が一度だけ放送され、その後に設問が続きます。問題用紙の設問と選択肢を読み、4つの選択肢の中から最も適切なものを選ぶ問題です。

・会話は印刷されていません。

・13の会話に3つの設問があるので、Part 3全体で39問です。

・3つの設問のうちの1つが、以下の形式になっているものがあります。

　　　1. 図表・グラフ問題形式：会話の中で聞いたことと問題用紙に印刷された図やグラフで見た情報を関連づけて解答します。

　　　2. 発言の意図を問う形式：クォーテーションマーク（引用符）部分の意味について解答します。

Step 2 Strategy（戦略）

◆ PREVIEW（準備）　解答用紙を開いたら…

音声を聞く前に3つの設問に目を通します。

　設問と選択肢が問題用紙に印刷されているので、音声を聞く前に3つの質問に素早く目を通しておくことで、聞こえてくる会話の内容の推測が可能です。

　3つの質問のうちの1つが、「図表・グラフ形式」のものや、「発言の意図」を問うものがあります。このような場合には、図表・グラフ、クォーテーションマーク部分にも素早く目を通します。そうすることで、解答につながるヒントを事前に得ることができます。

◆ Vocabulary Warm-up

　次のページの Exercise を行う前に、同じような発音の単語の意味を確認しましょう。

　1～6の下線部に当てはまる単語を下の (A) ～ (F) の中から選んで、その記号を書き入れてください。

1. ＿＿＿ is another word for ocean.
2. ＿＿＿ means to put a person in a chair.
3. ＿＿＿ is the unit of reproduction of a flowering plant.
4. ＿＿＿ means something that is morally bad.
5. ＿＿＿ means to take a very small drink.
6. ＿＿＿ is the combination of "she" and "will."

(A) seat　　(B) seed　　(C) she'll　　(D) sea　　(E) sip　　(F) sin

● Exercise 1-52〜57

音声を聞く前に、設問と選択肢に目を通す演習です。
音声を聞き、それぞれの説明文が A か B のどちらの状況に対応するかを選んでください。
Vocabulary Warm-up で確認した6つの単語がそれぞれの説明文に含まれています。
(A) と (B) の選択肢も短い語句のものなので、設問だけでなく選択肢にもできるだけ目を通してください。

1. What are they doing?
  (A) planning a trip   (B) talking on a ship

    Ⓐ Ⓑ

2. Where will the president most likely go?
  (A) to the front seat of a car   (B) to the first row of the audience

    Ⓐ Ⓑ

3. Where does this conversation most likely take place?
  (A) in someone's yard   (B) at a restaurant

    Ⓐ Ⓑ

4. What is the speaker's main point?
  (A) wasting food is bad   (B) people should choose salads

    Ⓐ Ⓑ

5. What does the person want someone to do?
  (A) share a drink   (B) water the plants

    Ⓐ Ⓑ

6. What is the speaker unsure of?
  (A) the size of the window   (B) someone's schedule

    Ⓐ Ⓑ

Step3 Analysis（分析）

◖ Analysis 1 3つの設問について

Part 3 では各会話文に必ず3つの設問が付きます。3つの設問は、大きく以下の3つに分類され、ふつう1から3の順序で出題されます。
1. General（一般的な質問）
2. Specific（具体的な質問）
3. Inference（会話から推測する質問）

STOPLIGHT TOEIC concept

　３つの分類は、道路の青信号・黄信号・赤信号になぞらえて考えることができます。

　この信号の概念は、設問内容の難易度と関わりはありません。これは、設問を解くために必要な考え方を表したものです。

Green = 一般的な質問 （進め）

　この形式に属する質問

　Main idea questions（会話の本題に関する質問）

　Scene-setting questions（場面設定に関する質問）

　Generalizing questions（一般論に関する質問）

　質問例

　Where are they?

　Who is the speaker?

　What are they mainly discussing?

Yellow = 具体的な質問 （注意）

　この形式に属する質問

　Exact location questions（正確な場所についての質問）

　Precise role questions（明確な役割についての質問）

　Specific reason questions（具体的な理由についての質問）

　質問例

　Where did the speaker say it happened?

　Why should listeners do X?

　Why is the speaker excited?

Red = 会話から推測する質問 （止まれ）

　この形式に属する質問

　Resulting action inference questions（結果として生じる行動の推測についての質問）

　Predicting course of action questions（予測される行動についての質問）

　Inferring choice/ decision questions（推測される選択 / 決定についての質問）

　質問例

　What will come next?

　Where will they go?

　What will they do?

　What will the speaker probably do next?

● Exercise 1

以下のそれぞれの質問が、Go (G) , Yield (Y), Stop (R) のどれに分類されるかを考え、表に
チェックマークを入れてください。

	Go (G) , Yield (Y), or Stop (R)?	GO	YIELD	STOP
1	Where most likely is this conversation taking place?			
2	What time does the next train leave?			
3	What will the man do next?			
4	Why is the coupon rejected?			
5	Where does the man suggest putting the table?			
6	What does the woman mean when says, "it's up to you?"			
7	What are the speakers mainly discussing?			
8	What does the woman suggest?			
9	What does the man agree to do?			
10	What is the woman asking about?			
11	When did they decide to meet?			

● Exercise 2

 1-58、59

では実際に2人の会話問題を解いてみましょう。

まず音声が流れる前に、次のページの3つの設問に目を通し内容を把握します。

実際の TOEIC 試験には、会話は印刷されていませんが、これは演習なので音声とともに会話
文を読んでください。

M: Could I see that silver bracelet on the second shelf?

W: Certainly. Here you go. It's actually 30 percent off, but the sale ends today.
It's only 385 dollars now! The regular price is 550 (five-fifty).

M: It's beautiful. I was thinking of getting something like this as an anniversary
present for my wife. Our anniversary is not for another 10 days, so I thought
I'd shop next week.

W: Well, as I said, today is the last day of our sale. Also, there's only one
bracelet left.

M: Ah, it sounds like I'd better get it today.

---

1. Where is the conversation taking place?
   (A) On the telephone
   (B) In a jewelry store
   (C) In a restaurant
   (D) In an office   Ⓐ Ⓑ Ⓒ Ⓓ

2. What extra information does the salesperson give the man?
   (A) The quantity of bracelets available
   (B) Where the bracelet was made
   (C) Another place to find the bracelet
   (D) The name of the bracelet designer   Ⓐ Ⓑ Ⓒ Ⓓ

3. Why will the man buy the bracelet today?
   (A) His anniversary is this week.
   (B) He wants his wife to have it right away.
   (C) He wants to get a better price.
   (D) He appreciates the good service.   Ⓐ Ⓑ Ⓒ Ⓓ

◖ Analysis 2   3人の会話問題

　Part 3 問題には、3人による会話文が含まれます。会話が複雑になるため、戸惑うことが多いのですが、非常に簡単かつ有効なアドバイスは以下のとおりです。

会話形式		課せられる質問
匿名の男性2名と女性1名	→	女性についてのもの
匿名の女性2名と男性1名	→	男性についてのもの

　なぜなら TOEIC では、「They（彼ら）」という形で3名についての質問はあっても、「A man and a woman（男性1名と女性1名）」についての質問や、「Two men（男性2名）」または「Two women（女性2名）」についての質問は発生しないからです。

では実際に 3 名による会話問題を解いてみましょう。

まず音声が流れる前に、 3 つの設問に目を通し内容を把握します。

実際の TOEIC 試験では、会話は印刷されていませんが、これは演習なので音声とともに会話文を読んでください。

M: Hey, Linda, have you been to the student cafeteria recently?

W1: No, not in months. I hate eating the same stuff over and over.

M: Well, I went yesterday and I was shocked. They have all sorts of international food now. I had a Korean plate that was actually pretty good!

W2: Uh..., Gary, sorry to listen in... you're talking about the new menu, right? I had a really nice meal there, too.

M: Something international?

W2: No... vegetable pasta... not pasta with vegetables, but pasta made from carrots and spinach!

M: I've heard about using zucchini to make noodles, but I've never tried it. Why don't we all go there for lunch today?

---

1. What are the speakers mainly discussing?

(A) Kinds of vegetables

(B) Cooking lessons

(C) Pasta making

(D) A new menu   Ⓐ Ⓑ Ⓒ Ⓓ

2. What does Gary say he's tried?

(A) A carrot salad

(B) A Korean plate

(C) Pasta made with vegetables

(D) Korean style carrots and spinach   Ⓐ Ⓑ Ⓒ Ⓓ

3. What does the man suggest they do?

(A) Get take-out

(B) Have a meal together

(C) Try another restaurant

(D) Order the Korean plate   Ⓐ Ⓑ Ⓒ Ⓓ

Analysis 3　図表付きの会話問題

2016年5月から、図表付きの設問が新たに加わりました。図や表は会話の内容に関連したものなので、音声が流れる前に、目を通しておくことで、会話自体の内容把握にも役立ちます。

● Exercise

 1-62、63

では実際に図表付きの会話問題を解いてみましょう。

まず音声が流れる前に、3つの設問に目を通し内容を把握します。

実際の TOEIC 試験には、会話は印刷されていませんが、これは演習なので音声とともに会話文を読んでください。

M: I'm concerned about the 3:00 P.M. slot in the schedule.

W: What's the problem?

M: There was just a huge article about Melissa Bronstein's company online that got thousands of hits. I think that we need to put her in a bigger room. Lots of people will want to go to her session.

W: Let's check the schedule sheet. Hmm... there are two rooms with twice the capacity.

M: Right, some of the rooms seat two times as many people.

W: I think we should switch her with this guy, because the woman in the other big room was the keynote speaker last year, so I'm guessing she'll attract a lot of people, too.

---

1. What are the speakers mainly discussing?

(A) The quality of the keynote speaker

(B) Who will introduce the speaker

(C) Issues with room size

(D) An issue with Ms. Bronstein's schedule　　Ⓐ Ⓑ Ⓒ Ⓓ

2. What does the man imply about Ms. Bronstein?

(A) She is very good at her job.

(B) Many will want to hear her speak.

(C) She is unhappy with the current schedule.

(D) She wants to deliver the keynote speech.　　Ⓐ Ⓑ Ⓒ Ⓓ

3:00 P.M. Concurrent Sessions

Speaker	Room #, Room Capacity	
Ms. Lisa McDonald	301	Seats 60
Mr. Peter Sato	303	Seats 60
Ms. Ronald Gomez	402	Seats 40
Ms. Melissa Bronstein	408	Seats 30

3. Look at the graphic. In which room will Ms. Bronstein most likely be speaking?

(A) 301

(B) 303

(C) 402

(D) 408   Ⓐ Ⓑ Ⓒ Ⓓ

Analysis 4　発言の意図を問う問題付きの会話問題

これも新形式の設問で、クォーテーションマーク部分の意味を推測して解答します。語句の意味は明白で直接的なものだけでなく、語句の持つニュアンスや暗示する意味の推測が必要なものもあります。設問は、通常、以下のような文章で始まります。

What does the man **mean** when he says, ...

What does the woman **imply** when she says, ...

● Exercise

1-64、65

では実際に発言の意図を問う問題付きの会話問題を解いてみましょう。

まず音声が流れる前に、3つの設問に目を通し内容を把握します。

実際の TOEIC 試験には、会話は印刷されていませんが、これは演習なので音声とともに会話文を読んでください。

W: I heard that you're unhappy with a new campus policy. May I ask what the trouble seems to be?

M: Yes. Actually, this whole thing is making me boiling mad... literally.

W: Ah...The school has asked us to turn the temperature up on the air conditioning, to save energy, so... I take it you're too hot?

M: Yeah. I just came out of a seminar with 10 people in our smallest classroom. If we can't turn the air conditioning down lower, keeping it on is pointless. We might as well open the windows and hope for a breeze.

W: Hmm... <u>Maybe they went a little overboard</u>. I'll make a few calls.

M: I really appreciate it.

1. What is the man concerned about?
   (A) Attendance at a recent seminar
   (B) An issue with the temperature
   (C) A window that does not open
   (D) A classroom that is too small   Ⓐ Ⓑ Ⓒ Ⓓ

2. What does the woman imply when she says, "Maybe they went a little overboard"?
   (A) She needs more information from the man.
   (B) She sees the man's point of view.
   (C) She spoke to some of the man's colleagues.
   (D) She needs to go to another seminar.   Ⓐ Ⓑ Ⓒ Ⓓ

3. What does the woman agree to do?
   (A) Contact people regarding the issue
   (B) Order new air conditioning equipment
   (C) Hold a seminar about the situation
   (D) Talk to the man again in the near future   Ⓐ Ⓑ Ⓒ Ⓓ

▶Mini Practice Test

◆ Part 3 （会話問題）

1-66〜73

設問の応答として最も適切な解答を選んでください。

1. 2人の会話

1. Who is the woman speaking to?
  (A) Her son
  (B) Her husband
  (C) A friend
  (D) A store clerk

Ⓐ Ⓑ Ⓒ Ⓓ

2. What is the woman willing to do to solve the problem?
  (A) Nothing
  (B) Send it herself
  (C) Pay extra
  (D) Shop somewhere else

Ⓐ Ⓑ Ⓒ Ⓓ

3. What will happen to the package?
  (A) It will get there a bit early.
  (B) It will still arrive late.
  (C) It will come exactly on time.
  (D) It will be shipped in 10 days.

Ⓐ Ⓑ Ⓒ Ⓓ

2. 3人の会話

4. What is the woman telling the men?
  (A) The hotel across the street is full.
  (B) Their wives must be worried about them.
  (C) A taxi is coming to take them home.
  (D) The weather is bad and they shouldn't go home.

Ⓐ Ⓑ Ⓒ Ⓓ

5. Why are they not driving home on alternate roads?
  (A) They are closed.
  (B) They are probably icy, too.
  (C) They like the hotel.
  (D) They are out of gas.

Ⓐ Ⓑ Ⓒ Ⓓ

6. Why is the woman going to the hotel with the men?

    (A) To stay, because she's not going home either

    (B) To show them the way

    (C) To help them check into their rooms

    (D) To wait in the lobby until the storm ends   Ⓐ Ⓑ Ⓒ Ⓓ

3. 図表付き

Friday April 30

Dentist	11:00	11:00	11:30	11:30
Arnold	✓		✓	✓
Furst	✓	✓	✓	
Granger	✓		✓	✓
Silverman	✓	✓		
Ito	✓		✓	✓

Attention Reception: You may schedule a maximum of two appointments per time slot per doctor.

7. Why did Justin call his dentist's office?

    (A) To talk to his dentist

    (B) To clean his teeth

    (C) To make an appointment for his son

    (D) To reschedule his appointment   Ⓐ Ⓑ Ⓒ Ⓓ

8. How is the new appointment different?

    (A) It is half an hour later.

    (B) It is one hour earlier.

    (C) It is one hour later.

    (D) It is half an hour earlier.   Ⓐ Ⓑ Ⓒ Ⓓ

9. Look at the graphic of the schedule from before the phone call. Which other dentist could have accommodated Justin's request?

    (A) Dr. Arnold

    (B) Dr. Furst

    (C) Dr. Granger

    (D) Dr. Ito   Ⓐ Ⓑ Ⓒ Ⓓ

4. 発言の意図を問う問題付き

10. Where is the party?

(A) At the woman's house

(B) At a retirement home

(C) At Steve Bennett's house

(D) At a nearby restaurant ⒶⒷⒸⒹ

11. What does the man need to bring to the party?

(A) Drinks

(B) Nothing

(C) Food

(D) Decoration ⒶⒷⒸⒹ

12. What does the woman imply when she says, "taken care of it"?

(A) She is handling Steve's health problems.

(B) She wants the man to be careful.

(C) She is not worried about the food and drink.

(D) She does not want the man to pay anything. ⒶⒷⒸⒹ

Part 4

Step1 Overview（概観）

◆ Format（構成）

・1人の話し手によるアナウンスやナレーションなどの説明文が1度だけ放送されます。

・説明文は印刷されていません。問題用紙の各説明文に関する設問と選択肢を読み、4つの選択肢の中から最も適切なものを選ぶ問題です。

・10 の説明文にそれぞれ3つの設問があるので、Part 4 全体で 30 問です。

・3つの設問のうちの1つが、以下の形式になっているものがあります。

　　1．図表・グラフ問題形式：会話の中で聞いたことと問題用紙に印刷された図やグラフで見た情報を関連づけて解答します。

　　2．発言の意図を問う形式：クォーテーションマーク部分の意味について解答します。

◆ Vocabulary Warm-up

以下の 18 個の単語に目を通してから、次ページの Vocabulary Match Part 1（リーディング）Part 2（リスニング）の演習を行ってください。

なお、これら 18 個の単語はすべて、本編で扱う説明文に用いられています。

1. slotted for　組み入れられる
2. hold　保留・電話を切らずに待つ
3. waiting time※ 待ち時間
4. installation　設置
5. accommodate　収容する
6. confirm　確認する
7. thriller　スリラー小説・映画
8. warranty　（商品の）保証書
9. guarantee　保証

10. annual　年次の
11. turn out　〜だと分かる
12. look forward　楽しみにする
13. refund　払い戻し・払戻す
14. retirement　退職
15. reschedule　再調整する
16. entitled to　〜の資格が与えられる
17. clearance　在庫一掃
18. hygienist　衛生士

※ waiting time は wait time と言い換えられます。

下の（A）を参考に、（B）〜（K）の空所に当てはまる語句を前ページの語彙リストから選び、その番号を書き入れてください。

1. If your ^(A) 8. warranty comes with a money-back ^(B)_____, you are（2 語）^(C)_____ _____ a full ^(D)_____.

2. We can only have 100 people in this room, so we can't ^(E)_____ all the invited guests here.

3. That clinic only has one dental ^(F)_____, in charge of all cleaning, so if you miss an appointment it takes a long time to ^(G)_____.

4. Every year, I（2 語）^(H)_____ _____ to the ^(I)_____ trip that the company usually has in May, but it（2 語）^(J)_____s _____ that it's（2 語）^(K)_____ _____ June this year, so I can't go.

Vocabulary Match **Part 2**

🔊 1-75〜79

5 つの短い文章を聞き、前ページの語彙リストの中から (L) 〜 (R) に当てはまる語句を選んでその番号を記入してください。

1. The speaker is discussing ^(L)_____ with some of the older workers.

2. The caller is being asked to ^(M)_____. The recording also lets the caller know how long the（2 語）^(N)_____ _____ is.

3. The speaker mentions that the ^(O)_____ was exciting.

4. The speaker is talking about a ^(P)_____ sale.

5. The caller wants to ^(Q)_____ that Mr. Steven's ^(R)_____ took place.

Step2 Strategy（戦略）

◆ PREVIEW（準備）　解答用紙を開いたら…

```
音声を聞く前に３つの設問に目を通します。
```

会話文（ダイアローグ）と説明文（モノローグ）の違いはありますが、設問形式は Part 3 と同様です。

設問と選択肢が問題用紙に印刷されているので、音声を聞く前に３つの設問に素早く目を通しておくことで、聞こえてくる会話の内容の推測が可能です。

３つの設問のうちの１つが、「図表・グラフ形式」のものや、「発言の意図」を問うものがあります。このような場合には、図表・グラフ、クォーテーションマーク部分にも素早く目を通します。そうすることで、解答につながるヒントを得ることができます。

Step3 | Analysis（分析）

⬤ Analysis 1 　STOPLIGHT TOEIC concept

Part 4 の設問も Part 3 と同様に、大きく以下の 3 つに分類され、概ね、1 から 3 の順序で出題されます。

General（一般的な質問）
　　青信号　Green = 一般的な質問。**GO**（進め）

Specific（具体的な質問）
　　黄色信号 Yellow = 細かい内容に関する質問。**YIELD**（注意）

Inference（会話から推測する質問）
　　赤信号　Red = 熟考、推測に関する質問。**STOP**（止まれ）

*設問形式は Part 3 と同じですから、ここで Unit 2 の STOPLIGHT TOEIC Concept のページを見直し確認してください。

⬤ Analysis 2 　頻出トピック

説明文としてよく出題されるジャンル、トピックは以下のとおりです。

ジャンル	例
アナウンス	オフィスビルの建設予定 空港でのフライト変更 スーパーやデパートでのセールス案内
TV やラジオの放送	ニュースレポート 天気予報 CM
スピーチ	受賞スピーチ 新任・退職の挨拶
ミーティング・セミナー	一般的な紹介—演説者、ゲスト、受賞者. グループメンバーを歓迎 ビジネスに関する話題の抜粋 販売統計・販売報告
電話（留守電）メッセージ	注文 個人的なメッセージ セールス 予約・予約の取り消し 予約変更（レストラン、病院、チケット等） イベントへの招待

● **Exercise**

では実際に Part 4 形式の問題を 2 問解いてみましょう。1 つはアナウンス、もう 1 つは留守番メッセージです。

分析のとおり、音声が流れる前に、設問と 4 つの選択肢に目を通し内容を把握しましょう。実際の TOEIC 試験には、スクリプトは印刷されていませんが、これは演習なので、音声とともにスクリプトを読んでください。

(1) アナウンス

Welcome to Leonardo's Pizza Palace. Our specials today include one large pizza and an order of chicken wings for $18.00 or two medium pizzas for $19.00. And remember, our daily special personal pizza is always just $12.00. We deliver to anywhere in the Fairfield area. We also have a restaurant on State Street. You can easily order there or place your name on the waiting list for dining in online at www.LeonardosPizza.net, too. If you would like to continue by phone, please hold and someone will be right with you. Thank you for choosing Leonardo's, where the food is reasonable, and the smiles are free!

---

1. What does the speaker imply when she says, "We also have a restaurant on State Street"?
(A) Delivery is preferable.
(B) It is possible to eat in.
(C) Delivery is cheaper.
(D) The restaurant is open late.

Ⓐ Ⓑ Ⓒ Ⓓ

2. How much is the least expensive special?
(A) $9.00   (B) $12.00
(C) $18.00   (D) $19.00

Ⓐ Ⓑ Ⓒ Ⓓ

3. What is suggested as a simple alternative?
(A) Calling back later
(B) Ordering wings and a large pizza
(C) Ordering online
(D) Getting two medium pizzas

Ⓐ Ⓑ Ⓒ Ⓓ

(2) 留守番メッセージ

Hello, Ms. Mulberg, this is Roy Jaworski calling from Knollwood Cable TV & Internet. We'd like to confirm your cable installation appointment scheduled for tomorrow, March 27th. You've been slotted for the afternoon, which means that a technician will visit between 1:00 and 5:00 P.M. It's necessary for someone over the age of 21 to be at home at the time of the installation. If you have any problem with this and need to make a different appointment, please call us before 7:00 P.M. this evening, March 26th. You can reach us at 877-555-2400. If the waiting time is long, we have a system that will automatically call you back. Thank you for choosing Knollwood Cable.

1. What type of service does the speaker's company perform?
   (A) It is a telephone company.
   (B) It is a media provider.
   (C) It is a machine repair service.
   (D) It provides firewood.

   Ⓐ Ⓑ Ⓒ Ⓓ

2. When is Ms. Mulberg's scheduled appointment?
   (A) The morning of the 21st
   (B) The evening of the 26th
   (C) The morning of the 27th
   (D) The afternoon of the 27th

   Ⓐ Ⓑ Ⓒ Ⓓ

3. What will Ms. Mulberg most likely do next?
   (A) Plan to be home for the installation
   (B) Call back Mr. Jaworski to confirm
   (C) Find out why her appointment was changed
   (D) Complain to customer service about the problem

   Ⓐ Ⓑ Ⓒ Ⓓ

Analysis **3** 図表付き

図や表は会話の内容に関連したものなので、音声が流れる前に、目を通しておくことで、会話自体の内容把握にも役立ちます。

● Exercise

CD 1-84、85

では実際に図表付きの問題を解いてみましょう。まず音声が流れる前に、3つの質問文に目を通し、質問内容を把握します。実際のTOEIC試験には、スクリプトは印刷されていませんが、これは演習なので、音声とともにスクリプトを読んでください。

Hi, this is Jenny calling from the National Sustainable Energy Society conference committee. We sent in our print order a little less than a week ago ... last Wednesday, but the conference is not for another two months, so I hope you haven't started printing yet. It turns out that the conference hotel restaurant will be able to accommodate another 100 people, so we'd like to ask you to print more tickets for us. If you have any questions about this, I can be reached at 617-555-1296, Jenny Hawkins. Actually, could you please call me back and confirm that you received this message? Thank you in advance.

Print Job: C7666340 National Sustainable Energy Society	Contact: J. Hawkins jhawkins@natsus.org
Item	Quantity
Name Badges with Logo (4 per sheet)	200
Conference Booklets	750
Conference Bags with Logo	725
Conference Dinner Tickets	500

1. What does the speaker say about the order?
   (A) She wants it by Wednesday.
   (B) She placed it last week.
   (C) She received it last Wednesday.
   (D) She wonders why it is late.

   Ⓐ Ⓑ Ⓒ Ⓓ

2. Look at the graphic. Which quantity on the original order form is no longer accurate?
   (A) 200   (B) 500
   (C) 720   (D) 750

   Ⓐ Ⓑ Ⓒ Ⓓ

3. What will the printer most likely do next?
   (A) Cancel this order   (B) Change the logo
   (C) E-mail Ms. Hawkins   (D) Call Ms. Hawkins back

   Ⓐ Ⓑ Ⓒ Ⓓ

◖ Analysis 4   発言の意図を問う問題付き

設問のクォーテーションマーク部分の意味を推測して解答します。語句の意味は明白で直接的なものだけでなく、語句の持つニュアンスや暗示する意味の推測が必要なものもあります。

● Exercise

🎧 1-86、87

では実際に発言の意図を問う問題付きの問題を解いてみましょう。まず音声が流れる前に、3つの設問に目を通し内容を把握します。実際の TOEIC 試験には、スクリプトは印刷されていませんが、これは演習なので音声とともにスクリプトを読んでください。

Hi, I'm Delilah Ramirez with this week's movie review. Last Friday, the new Craig Morris movie, *For Old Time's Sake,* opened. It's interesting to see Morris playing Clayton Winslow, an athlete who suddenly wakes up in an old man's body. I would have thought that Morris would be out of his element in a science fiction comedy. This film is totally unlike Morris's usual high drama thrillers. However, he manages to get big laughs over and over, as does his costar Janet Chan. Although the story is a bit predictable and the dialog feels quite young, watching this film is not a bad way for people of any age to spend a couple of hours.

1. What is the broadcast mainly about?
   (A) An analysis of a recent film
   (B) The career of a popular actor
   (C) The science used in a new movie
   (D) A remake of an old movie

   Ⓐ Ⓑ Ⓒ Ⓓ

2. What does the speaker say about the male lead?
   (A) His acting is quite bad.
   (B) He isn't as funny as the woman.
   (C) He doesn't usually play roles like this.
   (D) He plays an unsuccessful athlete.

   Ⓐ Ⓑ Ⓒ Ⓓ

3. What does the woman imply when she says, "would be out of his element"?
   (A) The writers should have adjusted the role to the actor.
   (B) She found the plot of the movie to be very basic.
   (C) She thought the actor would find the role difficult.
   (D) It is unexpected when the actor turns into a woman.

   Ⓐ Ⓑ Ⓒ Ⓓ

▶Mini Practice Test

◆ Part 4 （説明文問題）

 1-88〜93

説明文についての設問と4つの選択肢を読み，最も適切な解答を選んでください。

1.トーク

1. What is the main purpose of the talk?
(A) To thank the presenter for coming
(B) To inform the audience about sales numbers
(C) To give an orientation and talk about the speaker
(D) To explain how to give proper presentations   Ⓐ Ⓑ Ⓒ Ⓓ

2. According to the speaker, what are listeners expected to do?
(A) Respond to information in their handouts
(B) Discuss sales results in North and South America
(C) Give their evaluations of the speaker's presentation
(D) Collaborate with their team members   Ⓐ Ⓑ Ⓒ Ⓓ

3. What will the listeners hear next?
(A) Some words from the trainer
(B) What places to visit in South America
(C) What to write on their badges
(D) How to form some small groups   Ⓐ Ⓑ Ⓒ Ⓓ

2.図表付き

4. Why is Ms. Lopez calling?
(A) She wants to go out to dinner.
(B) She wants to eat at this restaurant.
(C) She needs some cooking advice.
(D) She hopes to get an adjustment.   Ⓐ Ⓑ Ⓒ Ⓓ

Creek River Mutual February 27 Dinner

Meal Type	Quantity
Chicken	25
Beef	32
Fish	18
Vegetarian	13

5. Look at the graphic. Which item is incorrect on this confirmation form?
(A) The beef meal
(B) The fish meal
(C) The chicken meal
(D) The vegetarian meal
Ⓐ Ⓑ Ⓒ Ⓓ

6. What does Ms. Lopez ask the listener to do?
(A) Return her call
(B) Check on ingredients
(C) Send another e-mail
(D) Cancel the order
Ⓐ Ⓑ Ⓒ Ⓓ

3. 発言の意図を問う問題付き

7. Who most likely is Ms. Morgan?
(A) A travel agent
(B) A new company employee
(C) An airline employee
(D) An insurance salesperson
Ⓐ Ⓑ Ⓒ Ⓓ

8. What does the speaker imply when he says, "you are entitled to a company discount"?
(A) The company can pay for insurance.
(B) Buying from North Star is a good idea.
(C) Everyone must get insurance today.
(D) Ms. Morgan needs to make a new plan.
Ⓐ Ⓑ Ⓒ Ⓓ

9. What will the listeners most likely do next?
(A) Answer the man's questions
(B) Listen to Ms. Morgan's talk
(C) Ask the man to explain further
(D) Visit Ms. Morgan's office
Ⓐ Ⓑ Ⓒ Ⓓ

Part 5

Part 5 短文穴埋め問題（Incomplete Sentences）

Step1 | Overview（概観）

◆ Format（構成）

・各文（25 ワード以内）は単語や語句が抜けており、その下に 4 つの選択肢が示されています。全 30 問で、文を完成させるのに最も適切な選択肢 (A) (B) (C) (D) の中から 1 つ選びます。

Step2 | Strategy（戦略）

◆ PREVIEW（準備）　解答用紙を開いたら…

●今まで習ってきた英文法をしっかり復習しましょう。

リーディングセクションの最初が Part 5 です。Part 5 は TOEIC テストの中でも最も学習し甲斐のあるセクションです。なぜなら、中学で学んだ文法を注意深く復習し、common grammar mistakes (英文法のよくある間違え) に注意を払えば、Part 5 のスコアは確実に伸びるからです。さらに頻出問題を反復し、頻出単語をこなせば全問正解も夢ではありません。

●文章は全部読みましょう。

　リーディングセクションは、 3 つのパートに分かれており、各パートで指示が与えられますが、75 分間に 100 問を解答する必要があります。中でも一番難しいのは様々な文章を短時間で読み、理解して解答しなければならない Part 7 です。
リーディンセクションでの時間配分を気にするあまり、Part 5 を空所の前後だけを読んで解答しようすると、意味を取り違えたりすることがありますから、文章は全部読むべきです。

●単語の接尾辞 (suffix) から品詞（parts of speech）を類推できます。

品詞（parts of speech）に注目すれば、Part 5 問題で空所に当てはまる単語を選び出す時間を短縮することができます。これは Part 6 でも有効なスキルです。
接尾辞 (suffix) と品詞の関連性

接尾辞	品詞		接尾辞	品詞
-ful	⇒ Aj（形容詞）		-fy	⇒ V （動詞）
-ly	⇒ Ad（副詞）		-ate	⇒ V （動詞）
-ion	⇒ N （名詞）			

◆ Vocabulary Warm-up

TASK 1

VAN の中には 20 の単語があり、接尾辞のセオリーが適用できる単語がかなり含まれています。単語の後の下線部分に、動詞は **V**、形容詞は **Aj**、副詞は **Ad**、そして名詞は **N** と書き込んでください。また、どの分類にも属さない単語が 1 つ含まれているので、そこには **X** と書き込んでください。

1. accurate __
2. application __
3. calculate __
4. carefully __
5. choice __
6. code __
7. cooperate __
8. corporate __
9. creation __
10. honor __
11. lavish __
12. mission __
13. moderately __
14. modify __
15. motivate __
16. passionate __
17. postpone __
18. template __
19. thoughtful __
20. without __

TASK 2

以下の各文章の下線部に、TASK 1 で品詞の分類をした単語の中からあてはまるものを選んで書き込んでください。1 から 11 に、形容詞、副詞、名詞、動詞に分類された単語が入ります。

Aj 下線部にあてはまる形容詞を選んで書き入れてください。
1. The _____ culture is very different from company to company.
2. You will see right away that John loves his work, as he is very _____ about this project.
3. I'd rather save money and go camping than have a _____ vacation at a resort.

Ad 下線部にあてはまる副詞を選んで書き入れてください。
4. Although he tries to express himself _____, he usually speaks too much.
5. Let's review your secondary school English grammar _____.

N 下線部にあてはまる名詞を選んで書き入れてください。
6. With each entrée you get your _____ of soup or salad.
7. The soldier said that doing her job well was a matter of _____.
8. The student made the slides using a colorful _____ he found online.

Ⅴ 下線部にあてはまる動詞を選んで書き入れてください。

9. The weather is supposed to be bad tomorrow, so we'll have to _____ the seminar.

10. More money is what companies use to _____ employees to work in hardship situations.

11. If you want peace, you need to get everyone involved to _____.

Step3 Analysis（分析）

Part 5 問題は「語彙」「品詞」「前置詞」「接続詞」「動詞」「代名詞」「関係詞」のほぼ 7 つのパターンに分類されます。

実際に、それぞれのパターンに分けて練習問題を解いてみましょう。

● Exercise

各文は単語や語句が抜けており、その下に 4 つの選択肢が示されています。文を完成するのに最も適切なものを 1 つずつ選んでください。

1 語彙問題 Vocabulary
異なる 4 つの語句から意味的に自然な選択肢を選んでください。

1. Having joined various clubs and taken part in non-academic activities can be ------ to students when they hunt for jobs.
   (A) beneficial   (B) relevant
   (C) convenient   (D) eligible
   Ⓐ Ⓑ Ⓒ Ⓓ

2. Increasing the number of female employees has been a strong goal of the company since it was first ------ last spring.
   (A) proposed   (B) offered
   (C) instructed   (D) removed
   Ⓐ Ⓑ Ⓒ Ⓓ

3. Ms. Guzman will make an announcement at the staff meeting regarding the details of the fifth floor ------ and how it will impact us.
   (A) connection   (B) demonstration
   (C) construction   (D) emotion
   Ⓐ Ⓑ Ⓒ Ⓓ

2 品詞問題 Parts of speech

名詞・動詞・形容詞・副詞など異なる役割を持つ語句から、もっとも適切な選択肢を選んでください。

1. The gathering was to be a ------ of the heroes involved in rescuing people during the recent disaster.

(A) celebrate   (B) celebrated

(C) celebrating   (D) celebration

Ⓐ Ⓑ Ⓒ Ⓓ

2. If you wish to have a positive influence on youth, you must act ------ in front of them.

(A) responsibility   (B) responsible

(C) responsibly   (D) responsiveness

Ⓐ Ⓑ Ⓒ Ⓓ

3. They have ------ the "Young Researchers" grant to include people under the age of 40, rather than 35.

(A) modify

(B) modifying

(C) modified

(D) modification

Ⓐ Ⓑ Ⓒ Ⓓ

3 前置詞問題 Prepositions

前置詞から、最も適切な選択肢を選んでください。

1. According to the guidebook, there is some famous, beautiful art in the old museum ------ State Street.

(A) at   (B) of

(C) on   (D) by

Ⓐ Ⓑ Ⓒ Ⓓ

2. We learned about Mr. Jackson's talents ------ his supervisor and contacted him about our project.

(A) by   (B) with

(C) through   (D) over

Ⓐ Ⓑ Ⓒ Ⓓ

4 接続詞問題 Conjunctions

接続詞から最も適した語句を選んでください。

1. ------ nobody else volunteered to help with the event, Bob found himself staying at the help desk the entire time.
   (A) And
   (B) Since
   (C) Yet
   (D) So

   Ⓐ Ⓑ Ⓒ Ⓓ

2. Please check for errors in any of your personal information ------ you get the document by e-mail attachment.
   (A) by
   (B) until
   (C) in case
   (D) as soon as

   Ⓐ Ⓑ Ⓒ Ⓓ

5 動詞問題 Verbs

進行形・受動態、時制など、動詞の最も適した形を選んでください。

1. Until the attack, government officials ------ in that bistro dozens of times without security issues.
   (A) had eaten
   (B) have eaten
   (C) was eating
   (D) will have eaten

   Ⓐ Ⓑ Ⓒ Ⓓ

2. The research that Dr. Black ------ to cite in the patent application was recently discredited.
   (A) intend
   (B) will intend
   (C) have intended
   (D) was intending

   Ⓐ Ⓑ Ⓒ Ⓓ

6　代名詞問題 Pronouns

代名詞の中からもっとも適切な選択肢を選んでください。

1. It is standard procedure that websites asking for personal information from consumers inform them of ------ privacy protection policy.

(A) their

(B) they

(C) them

(D) its

Ⓐ Ⓑ Ⓒ Ⓓ

2. ------ of the candidates had the exact qualifications that the search committee was looking for in a new CEO.

(A) No one

(B) None

(C) Almost

(D) Some

Ⓐ Ⓑ Ⓒ Ⓓ

7　関係詞問題　(relative pronouns)

関係詞の中からもっとも適切な選択肢を選んでください。

1. Mr. Higgin's promotion to general manager was no surprise to those ------ worked with him.

(A) who

(B) whom

(C) whoever

(D) whomever

Ⓐ Ⓑ Ⓒ Ⓓ

2 The supplement company started a program ------ provides significant discounts to customers who place monthly orders or order in bulk.

(A) what

(B) where

(C) when

(D) which

Ⓐ Ⓑ Ⓒ Ⓓ

▶Mini Practice Test

◆ Part 5 （短文穴埋め問題）

4つの選択肢の中から空所に最も適切なものを１つ選んでください。

1. When Leo entered the university, he planned to major ------ politics, but he decided to become a sociologist, instead.

   (A) of   (B) in

   (C) for   (D) on

   Ⓐ Ⓑ Ⓒ Ⓓ

2. ------ the students were able to get a passing grade on the test, even though it was the most difficult one in many years.

   (A) Almost   (B) Almost all

   (C) Even   (D) Even all

   Ⓐ Ⓑ Ⓒ Ⓓ

3. The Art Department is asking for ------ on new logo designs, so please answer the survey questions regarding their drafts.

   (A) feedback

   (B) pushback

   (C) comeback

   (D) kickback

   Ⓐ Ⓑ Ⓒ Ⓓ

4. The coach encouraged the players to support each other on the field in order to finish the season ------ .

   (A) helpfully

   (B) hopefully

   (C) successfully

   (D) truthfully

   Ⓐ Ⓑ Ⓒ Ⓓ

5. Hoping to be selected for a position in the foreign service, Kate ------ both Chinese and Korean for the last few years.

   (A) was studying

   (B) studied

   (C) has been studying

   (D) will study

   Ⓐ Ⓑ Ⓒ Ⓓ

6. You can still get into the program if you turn in your ------ by next Thursday.
(A) apply
(B) application
(C) applying
(D) applied

Ⓐ Ⓑ Ⓒ Ⓓ

7. The youth center is a place ------ all young people, regardless of the neighborhood they come from, can enjoy playing sports and games together.
(A) when
(B) where
(C) which
(D) whom

Ⓐ Ⓑ Ⓒ Ⓓ

8. That bird is known for ------ bright red body and white markings on the tail.
(A) it
(B) its
(C) their
(D) them

Ⓐ Ⓑ Ⓒ Ⓓ

9. I would like to ------ that you ask for some volunteers to work on restoring the school garden to its former glory.
(A) offer
(B) prevent
(C) protest
(D) suggest

Ⓐ Ⓑ Ⓒ Ⓓ

10. Sandy decided to put a sign up in the hallway ------ that nobody would slip on the wet floor.
(A) as
(B) so
(C) for
(D) but

Ⓐ Ⓑ Ⓒ Ⓓ

Part 6

Part 6 長文穴埋め問題（Text Completion）

Step1 Overview（概観）

◆ Format（構成）

- ・各文書の中で、単語や語句または一文が抜けており、文書の下にそれぞれの空所に対応する4つの選択肢が示されています。文書を完成させるのに最も適切な選択肢を選び、(A) (B) (C) (D) のいずれかを選びます。
- ・1文書につき4問 x 4セットで、全16問です。
- ・文章のジャンルは、論文要旨、方針概略、電子メール、通知、手紙などで、いずれも概ね150単語以内です。文章の中に4つの下線部があり、文法力、語彙力、そして語彙や文章の文脈における理解力が試されます。

Step2 Strategy（戦略）

◆ PREVIEW（準備） 解答用紙を開いたら…

●急がば回れ！文章全体を読み、文脈に基づいて設問を解く。

文章の中に4つの空所があり、1つは文章形式で、残りはPart 5形式です。
文章形式の設問は文章全体を読まないと解答できません。
Part 5形式の設問は、空所の前後や空所を含む文章だけ読めば、解答できるものもありますが、実際には文脈の中から判断しないと解けない設問も含まれています。「ここは読み飛ばし」「ここはじっくり読む」と考えていると、内容を読み違える可能もあり、かえって効率が悪くなります。

●急がば回れ！英文速読術は用いない

複数の長文を読んで解答するPart 7では、スキミング（文章の要点をすくい取り、全体の大意を理解する）やスキャンニング（大量の文章から特定の情報を探し出す）といった英文速読術が用いられることもありますが、Part 6はスキミングやスキャンニングが有効になるほどの文章量ではありません。Part 6では特に文章形式の設問においては、英文速読術は避けるべきです。

●消去法─文脈から外れるような選択肢を除外する

前述のとおり、Part 6 では文脈を追って正しい文の流れを見定めることが求められます。鍵となる情報を読み飛ばさないように気を配る必要があります。

文章にはまとまりがあり、基本的に唐突にトピックから外れるようなことはないので、本筋から外れるような選択肢を排除していきましょう。この "Process of elimination（消去法）" は、文章形式の設問だけでなく Part 5 形式の語彙問題でも効果的です。

◆ Vocabulary Warm-up

TASK 1

VAN の中には 18 の単語があり、接尾辞のセオリーが適用できる単語も含まれています。単語の後の下線部分に、動詞は V、形容詞は Aj、副詞は Ad、そして名詞は N と書き込んでください。また、どの分類にも属さない単語が 2 つ含まれているので、そこには X と書き込んでください。

接尾辞 (suffix) と品詞の関連性

接尾辞		品詞	接尾辞		品詞
-ful	⇒	Aj（形容詞）	-ly	⇒	Ad（副詞）
-ion	⇒	N（名詞）	-fy	⇒	V（動詞）
-ate	⇒	V（動詞）			

注）Unit 4 の TASK でも行ったとおり、通常 -ly で終わる単語は副詞に分類されます。しかし時として、形容詞として使われることもあります。-ly が形容詞として使われている単語が以下の VAN には含まれていますので注意してください。

1. adequate ___   7. coincidence ___   13. modestly ___
2. anticipate ___   8. corporation ___   14. mystery ___
3. cancel ___   9. creatively ___   15. notify ___
4. casually ___   10. honorable ___   16. permanent ___
5. chore ___   11. lovely ___   17. through ___
6. choose ___   12. minimum ___   18. without ___

TASK 2

前ページの語彙リストの中から下線部に文脈に沿って当てはまる単語を選んで書き入れてください。

1. This is not the best room for your art as it doesn't get _____ light.
2. When you _____ an apartment, you should consider facilities, convenience and price.
3. She found out about the job _____ an online advertisement.
4. Emma likes her job, but at first she was worried about working for such a big _____ .
5. The contract is for three years, so Steve's job is not _____ .
6. Mr. Ho asked us to keep our party budget to the absolute _____ , so we can't buy much.
7. Jose bumped into his teacher at the movies theater and thought it was quite a _____ that they were there at the same time.

Step3 | Analysis（分析）

次の文章を読んでください。各段落に、単語や語句または一文が抜けているところがあります。

Press Release

Brain Gym 2 Go, BG2G, is a new educational toy to help stimulate young minds. Made of flexible materials, it can easily be __問 1__ to any place your baby uses.

Before going to sleep, the baby can enjoy it in the crib or in the stroller, while __問 2__ a walk.

The baby can __問 3__ it on the road—just clip it to the car seat. While you are shopping, you can even put it on the shopping cart.

The BG2G attaches to almost any surface in seconds. And, best of all, the BG2G is easy to maintain. __問 4__ Call 1-800-555-3900 to find out how to get yours.

⬤ Analysis 1　タイトル

　文章にタイトルがあれば、それは内容を推測する鍵になります。この場合は Press Release（報道発表）ですから、新商品の紹介、政府などによる記事発表などが考えられます。文章が E メールであれば、差出人や宛先人の名前、件名などから内容が推測できます。

⬤ Analysis 2　問題形式

前ページの Press Release を参照しながら、次の設問を解いてください。

文法問題
　問 1 では、空欄の前後（be と to）の間に入るのはどれかを、問 2 では、while の後に続く動詞はどの形をとるかを見極めます。

問 1　(A) attach
　　　(B) to attach
　　　(C) attached
　　　(D) attaching

問 2　(A) take
　　　(B) taking
　　　(C) to take
　　　(D) taken

語彙問題
　どの動詞が文脈の中で最も自然かを考えます。

問 3　(A) use　　　　　　　(B) fix
　　　(C) perform　　　　　(D) satisfy

文章問題
　4 つの文の中でどれが、この段落の内容に合っているかを判断します。

問 4
　(A) Nonetheless, be careful not to put BG2G close to where the baby sleeps.
　(B) Just wipe BG2G clean with a damp cloth or put it in the washing machine.
　(C) However, the activities on BG2G are somewhat difficult to do while moving.
　(D) These are just a few of the color and design choices available for BG2G.

● **Exercise**

最後に次の問題を解いてください。

OPENING CELEBRATION
Garden Fresh, 2954 Warren Place, Greenfield
May 5, 5:00–10:00 P.M.

You are invited to the **OPENING CELEBRATION** of a new restaurant committed
to serving fresh, local and ----1.---- food. All of the produce, the fruit, vegetables,
and herbs served at **Garden Fresh** are grown on the restaurant grounds.

There will be two seatings for the **OPENING CELEBRATION**, the first at 5:00
P.M. and the second at 7:30. Diners will have the ----2.---- to sample Chef Samuel's
unique creations. To begin with, brief, pre-seating garden tours will be
conducted by Master Gardener Regina Cardini, who will also offer a few handy
tips for managing a successful garden. ----3.---- .
All guests will receive a raffle ticket and there will be a drawing for a free
dinner-for-two certificate at 6:30. The dinner certificate must be ----4.---- within
three months.

---

1. (A) season   (B) seasons
   (C) seasonal   (D) seasoning

   Ⓐ Ⓑ Ⓒ Ⓓ

2. (A) flavor   (B) resources
   (C) responsibility   (D) opportunity

   Ⓐ Ⓑ Ⓒ Ⓓ

3. (A) The tour bus will depart immediately after each group finishes their dinner.
   (B) Ms. Samuel will then answer questions about the garden.
   (C) The tours will be followed by a chance to enjoy the chef's choice.
   (D) Ms. Cardini will demonstrate European cooking techniques after the tours.

   Ⓐ Ⓑ Ⓒ Ⓓ

4. (A) used   (B) substituted
   (C) returned   (D) consumed

   Ⓐ Ⓑ Ⓒ Ⓓ

▶Mini Practice Test

◆ Part 6 （長文穴埋め問題）

文章を読んで、空所に入るのに最も適切なものを選んでください。

Notice to all county residents:

Hurricane season is ---1.--- us, so this is a good time to make sure you are ready at home. Here are some tips for better storm and disaster preparedness. Stock an emergency kit with enough canned/packaged food and water for at least five days. Include a flashlight, first aid supplies, cash and important documents, such as passports, and insurance cards. ---2.---

The day before the storm bring in, or tie down, outdoor furniture and any items that could blow away. Bookmark local government and weather websites so that you have ---3.--- access to storm updates and emergency instructions. Twelve hours before the hurricane, check news and government websites for the ---4.--- weather updates. Charge your cell phone; you'll want to have a full battery if the power goes out.

---

1. (A) at   (B) upon
   (C) over   (D) to   Ⓐ Ⓑ Ⓒ Ⓓ

2. (A) Cover windows outside with wood and tape, the inside in an X-shape.
   (B) Contact local officials informing them that you are prepared and will not need emergency help.
   (C) Call close friends to determine their exact location during the storm.
   (D) Have a plan for communicating with family members if you lose power or become separated.
                                                        Ⓐ Ⓑ Ⓒ Ⓓ

3. (A) ease   (B) easy
   (C) eased   (D) easily   Ⓐ Ⓑ Ⓒ Ⓓ

4. (A) fastest   (B) latest
   (C) finest   (D) longest   Ⓐ Ⓑ Ⓒ Ⓓ

Paid Internship Available

Marsten Business Solutions is searching for someone in the ----5.---- of marketing. Four to eight-week internships are available during standard college spring, summer and winter breaks. No experience is ----6.---- , but previous study in the areas of economics or business is preferred. In addition to filling out the online application at www.marstenbiz.com/internship, you are asked to upload a short essay to the site, as per the instructions, ----7.---- a live interview. Subsequently, our hiring committee will be video-conferencing with all applicants that make our short list. Celine Abernathy is happy to answer any questions you may have. Please e-mail her at cabernathy@marstenbiz.com. Our goal is reach out to those interested in a future in marketing. ----8.---- .

5. (A) globe   (B) land

   (C) place   (D) world   Ⓐ Ⓑ Ⓒ Ⓓ

6. (A) necessity   (B) necessary

   (C) necessitated   (D) necessarily   Ⓐ Ⓑ Ⓒ Ⓓ

7. (A) in the hopes of   (B) in place of

   (C) in relation to   (D) in proportion to   Ⓐ Ⓑ Ⓒ Ⓓ

8. (A) So, let us know if you do not have reliable internet access.

   (B) We apologize for the short turn-around time in this notice.

   (C) So, please share this information with possible candidates.

   (D) Please make sure you already have a strong background in business.

                                                  Ⓐ Ⓑ Ⓒ Ⓓ

To: Mr. Martin Gonzalez
Fremont Business Consultant Group

Dear Martin,

As I mentioned to you the other day, ---9.--- our system to clients is a major part of our business, yet the ---10.--- skills level of our employees is quite weak. I understand that you have conducted seminars on how to give the most ---11.--- presentations and that you would be willing to work with our staff.

Our budget for your work that day would need to be $375. I know that you usually receive between $400-500 per day for your services out of town, but, as we are located right near your office, it should be a situation where you would not need to devote a lot of time to travel. ---12.--- .

Thank you for considering this.
Alison Murphy

9. (A) demonstrating   (B) demonstrate
   (C) demonstration   (D) demonstrated   Ⓐ Ⓑ Ⓒ Ⓓ

10. (A) present   (B) presented
    (C) presentation   (D) presently   Ⓐ Ⓑ Ⓒ Ⓓ

11. (A) effect   (B) affected
    (C) effective   (D) affecting   Ⓐ Ⓑ Ⓒ Ⓓ

12. (A) Please speak to Margaret Sasaki if you agree to these conditions.
    (B) You would need to pay a few weeks in advance to take part in the seminar.
    (C) Please estimate your travel costs for the seminar and let us know.
    (D) Once you accept, we will assign someone to be in charge of your training.

                                                           Ⓐ Ⓑ Ⓒ Ⓓ

Unit 6 Part 7

Part 7 読解問題（シングルパッセージ） （マルチプルパッセージ）

Step1 Overview（概観）

◆ Format（構成）

シングルパッセージ　　　　　　　　（設問　各2問〜4問）　　　29問
　　　　普通の文
　　　　テキストメッセージ

マルチプルパッセージ　　　　　　　（設問　各5問）　　　　　25問
　　　　ダブルパッセージ
　　　　トリプルパッセージ

Step2 Strategy（戦略）

●長文読解の鍵は「設問」に

Part 7は多量の英文を読み、全部で54問もの設問に解答しなければならない難易度が高いセクションです。これまでParts 1-4（リスニング・セクション）そしてParts 5, 6（リーディング・セクション）を解いてきた後では集中力の維持にも苦労しますし、残り時間のプレッシャーもあります。

こうした状況の中では、やみくもに本文を読み始めても内容が頭に入ってきません。まずは落ち着いて、設問に目を通しましょう。本文のどんな内容についての解答が求められているのかを把握しておくことが重要となるため、できるだけ多くの設問形式を演習し、設問の意図を的確に把握できるようになることが、スコアを向上させる効果的な方法です。

Step3 Analysis（分析）

Analysis 1　シングルパッセージ

1つの文章を読み、内容に関する2〜4つの設問に答える形式です。普通の文章のものと、テキストメッセージのものがあります。いずれも、文章自体はさほど長くありませんが、各文章に対する設問を連続して解く必要があります。

シングルパッセージには、設問の1つが以下の形式になっているものがあります。

1. 文中の語句の意味を選ぶ問題（語彙問題）
2. 一文を入れる適切な位置を選ぶ問題（文章問題）

● Exercise 1

　以下のエクササイズで、設問形式を読み解く演習をしてみましょう。このエクササイズは、「シングルパッセージ設問2」タイプのものですが、それぞれの設問に対して、2通りの設問が用意されています。

　ひとつの文章に対して、2通りの設問を演習することで、この文章に対する理解を深めることができるでしょう。

Double Time Warm-up

Morganstern Promotions
Hi Delilah

—[1]— I'd really like to introduce you to all of our department heads. If we can **time** such a meeting to occur when you are in town next week, the schedule would be perfect.

One of our main clients has a new film opening next Friday, as well. I was hoping that we could **catch** either a matinee or evening showing. I'd like to introduce you to Mr. Matthews, the man who directed the film. —[2]—

We also have meetings scheduled with a fast food company that will be offering a tie-in product for children featuring characters from the movie. —[3]— All of this should give you a good idea of the kind of work we do. —[4]—

1　語彙問題

文中で使われている2つの単語について、同じ意味を持つものを選んでください。

　1. time

　　(A) arrange

　　(B) compute the minutes of

　　(C) hit

　　(D) measure the speed of

　　　　　　　　　　　　　　　　　　　　Ⓐ Ⓑ Ⓒ Ⓓ

2. catch

　(A) attach

　(B) attend

　(C) capture

　(D) understand　　　　　　　　　　　　　　　　Ⓐ Ⓑ Ⓒ Ⓓ

2 文章問題

[1]、[2]、[3]、[4] と記載された箇所のうち、次の文が入るのに最もふさわしいのはどれですか。

　1. "I've heard that you are coming to LA."

　　(A) [1]

　　(B) [2]

　　(C) [3]

　　(D) [4]　　　　　　　　　　　　　　　　　　　Ⓐ Ⓑ Ⓒ Ⓓ

　2. "The director would like to accompany us to the theater."

　　(A) [1]

　　(B) [2]

　　(C) [3]

　　(D) [4]　　　　　　　　　　　　　　　　　　　Ⓐ Ⓑ Ⓒ Ⓓ

● **Exercise** 2

テキストメッセージ

設問の意図に留意しながら、次のテキストメッセージ形式問題を解いてみましょう。

Questions 1-2 refer to the following text message chain.

Walter Ramirez　　　　[12:50 P.M.]

I brought the handouts… Student orientation starts at 1:30.
Let's meet outside the lecture hall at 1:15.

Sharon Kang　　　　[12:55 P.M.]

Okay. I should be there just after 1:00.

Walter Ramirez　　　　[1:10 P.M.]

Where are you? I'm in front of Room 310, but they're all engineering
students waiting in the hall, not education majors.

Sharon Kang	[1:11 P.M.]
Didn't you get the e-mail about the room change?	

Walter Ramirez	[1:12 P.M.]
Guess not...	

Sharon Kang	[1:12 P.M.]
We're in 102.	

Sharon Kang	[1:13 P.M.]
I may have forgotten to forward that message. Sorry...	

Walter Ramirez	[1:14 P.M.]
It's all good. Be there in a few minutes.	

Sharon Kang	[1:15 P.M.]
The previous session is just letting out. I'll set up.	

Walter Ramirez	[1:15 P.M.]
OK.	

1. What is suggested about Mr. Ramirez and Ms. Kang?
   (A) They are meeting for the first time at orientation.
   (B) They were both unaware of the room change.
   (C) They are working together today.
   (D) They both arrived late for orientation.

   Ⓐ Ⓑ Ⓒ Ⓓ

2. At 1:14, what does Mr. Ramirez mean when he writes, "It's all good"?
   (A) He is not concerned about the presentation.
   (B) He knows he can find the room.
   (C) He accepts Ms. Kang's apology.
   (D) He agrees to discuss the issue later.

   Ⓐ Ⓑ Ⓒ Ⓓ

◑ Analysis 2　ダブルパッセージ、トリプルパッセージ

　ダブルパッセージでは２つの文章を、トリプルパッセージでは３つの関連する文章を読み、それぞれ内容に関する５つの設問に答えます。

　ダブルパッセージでは１つ目の文章と２つ目の文章の両方を読まないと解けない問題が出題されることがありますし、トリプルパッセージでは、設問１が文章２、設問２が文章１と２、設問３が文章２と３、設問４が文章３、設問５が文章１…といった具合に、特定の文章を飛ばしてヒントが出たり、３つの文章を参照しないと解けない設問が出題されることもあります。

　ただし、ダブルパッセージでも、トリプルパッセージでも、本文と設問の順番は、一致することが多く、また最初の設問は１つ目の文章から出題される傾向が高いので、まず１つ目の設問を読んでから、１つ目の文章に目を通す、そして２つ目の設問…といったやり方を試しましょう。

● Exercise

では、実際にトリプルパッセージの問題を解いてみましょう。

Questions 1-5 refer to the following email, menu and review.

Name: customergroup@littlepariscafe.co.ca
Date: April 22
Subject: Customer Appreciation Month

Dear Friend,

We wish to express our gratitude for your continued support. We at Little Paris Café would like to reward your loyalty. The month of May is customer appreciation month. Either bring a hard copy of this e-mail or show the message to the host on your phone and this will serve as a reusable coupon for $8 off all dinner specials and $5 off lunch specials.

Reusable means the coupon may be utilized by each member of your party, and as many times as you'd like throughout May. Please be advised that starting May 1, only the trout, tuna, sole, steak and chicken will be available at lunch time.

Thank you again, and I look forward to welcoming you here soon.

Angela Romanoff, Chef

Little Paris Café Specials

Appetizers

- Asparagus and Mushroom Medley
- Spinach Puffs
- Whitefish Mousse
- Blue Cheese Salad

Fish

- Sautéed Dover Sole
- Seared Tuna Steak
- Grilled Trout
- French-style Seafood Stew

Meat

- Herb-crusted Lamb Chops
- T-bone Steak
- Prime Rib
- Roasted Chicken

Lunch Special-- Choice of one appetizer and fish or meat dish $19
Dinner Special-- Choice of one appetizer, one fish and one meat dish $32
All sets include torte of the day and coffee or tea.
(Specials do not include tax, gratuity or beverage charges.)

Restaurant Review

May21

★★★⯪☆

I recently dined at Little Paris Café for lunch. As an e-mail list recipient, I was able to enjoy a discount for customer appreciation month. I chose the blue cheese salad and grilled trout for my meal. The salad was a bit on the small side, but the trout was tasty. Unfortunately, the fish special I wanted to order was not being served. Also, I thought that the service was much slower than it had been in the past. Perhaps I was more conscious of this because I was dining alone and hoping to be able to get in and out quickly, but that was not the case.

Gregory Benson

1. What is the purpose of the e-mail?

    (A) to introduce a new chef

    (B) to offer special discounts

    (C) to announce new menu items

    (D) to explain changes in hours

        Ⓐ Ⓑ Ⓒ Ⓓ

2. The word "serve" in the 4th line of the first paragraph of the e-mail is closest in meaning to

    (A) distribute

    (B) supply

    (C) be used

    (D) be helped

        Ⓐ Ⓑ Ⓒ Ⓓ

3. Which is NOT different between lunch and dinner?

    (A) The overall price of the meal

    (B) The selection of appetizers

    (C) The number of dishes served

    (D) The amount of the discount

        Ⓐ Ⓑ Ⓒ Ⓓ

4. What does Mr. Benson indicate he would have preferred to order?

    (A) Seared Tuna Steak

    (B) French-style Seafood Stew

    (C) Herb-crusted Lamb Chops

    (D) Prime Rib

        Ⓐ Ⓑ Ⓒ Ⓓ

5. What did Mr. Benson's meal cost before tax and tip?

    (A) $14

    (B) $19

    (C) $24

    (D) $32

        Ⓐ Ⓑ Ⓒ Ⓓ

▶Mini Practice Test

◆ Part 7 （読解問題）

文章について設問と選択肢を読んで、解答として最も適切なものを選んでください。

Questions 1-2 refer to the following text message chain.

Thelma Dirks   [8:24 P.M.]
Hi Glenn. Looking forward to seeing all you Baltimore folks at tomorrow's conference in Chicago. Do you arrive early enough to meet for dinner?

Glenn Masuda   [8:26 P.M.]
Actually, just me this time. I should check in by 6:00 at the latest.

Thelma Dirks   [8:27 P.M.]
I'm on a 2:00 flight, so I land at 3:40. I need to pick up my bags and grab a cab, but I should be at the hotel by 5:00.

Glenn Masuda   [8:29 P.M.]
Wait, my flight gets in at 3:15. I'm planning to rent a car. I could hang out at baggage claim and we could drive to the hotel together.

Thelma Dirks   [8:31 P.M.]
Seriously? I'm on Southeast Airways FLT 203. Why don't I text you when I land?

Glenn Masuda   [8:32 P.M.]
Sounds like a plan. See you tomorrow.

---

1. What does Mr. Masuda mean when he writes, "just me this time"?

(A) This is something he can handle alone.

(B) He does not want to miss the conference.

(C) The problem with sales is his fault.

(D) He is attending the event by himself.

Ⓐ Ⓑ Ⓒ Ⓓ

2. What does Ms. Dirks imply by her suggestion to text Mr. Masuda?

(A) She wants to keep him informed.

(B) She likes the choice of hotel.

(C) She plans to work on the plane.

(D) She wishes to accept his offer.

Ⓐ Ⓑ Ⓒ Ⓓ

Questions 3-6 refer to the following memorandum.

Memorandum

February 15

To: all staff

We would like to welcome our new Chief Creative Officer (CCO), Michelle Berkowitz, to Atlas Atlanta Advertising. Ms. Berkowitz hails from Denver, where she started as a copywriter at Wilco Promotion. —[1]— She has more than 25 years in the business and has been in charge of dozens of national campaigns for major corporations including Parson's Potato Chips and Claymore Insurance. —[2]—

We will be holding a special reception for Michelle at the Carleton-Ambassador Hotel on March 27 at 7:30 P.M. —[3]— Your spouse or significant other is also invited. —[4]— Please RSVP to your department head by March 5 and indicate the name of your plus-one, if you will be bringing someone.

We look forward to seeing you there.

Marilyn Wong, CEO

---

3. What is the purpose of the memorandum?

(A) To promote a new advertising campaign

(B) To announce Ms. Wong's arrival at the firm

(C) To offer employees hotel discounts

(D) To invite people to a welcome party

Ⓐ Ⓑ Ⓒ Ⓓ

4. In paragraph 1, line 2, the word "hails" is close in meaning to

(A) calls

(B) comes

(C) greets

(D) stops

Ⓐ Ⓑ Ⓒ Ⓓ

5. Who is the event for?

(A) Executives and spouses

(B) Executives and department heads

(C) All staff

(D) A new CCO

Ⓐ Ⓑ Ⓒ Ⓓ

6. In which of the positions marked [1], [2], [3], and [4] does the following sentence best belong? "She is also the recipient of the Advertisers' Guild 2017 Best Ad Campaign award."

(A) [1]

(B) [2]

(C) [3]

(D) [4]

Ⓐ Ⓑ Ⓒ Ⓓ

Questions 7-11 are based on the following online review and response.

Review

Lotus Wrist Support Gloves ✳ ✳

I have been wearing wrist supports for many years. I like to bowl and participate in other activities and sports that put a strain on my wrists. I was attracted to the gloves because the price was lower than most, but it seems that the quality is lower as well. I thought they were helping a bit, so I was initially satisfied, but after less than a month, the stitching completely came apart on the left one. As I am right-handed, I don't think I was overusing this item at all. I only wear them in the afternoon and early evening when I am actively pursuing my hobbies.

Response from the Manufacturer

Customerservice@lotussupports.com

We are sorry to hear about your experience with the gloves. You have obviously received a defective pair. On rare occasions problems such as what you have experienced occur. If you contact us directly at the above e-mail address, we will replace your item at no charge. In your correspondence, please indicate your name, address, the place of purchase, purchase price and size of the gloves in your message.

You have drawn an incorrect conclusion about our gloves. Keeping our gloves reasonable is out of respect to our repeat customers. Gloves are not a long-term investment and do have to be replaced. We are trying to be conscious of the budget of our consumers. We pride ourselves on the materials that we use.

Actually, our return rate has been less than 3% over the past 10 years. It is quite unusual for a product to degrade in such a short period of time. We will look into this matter. In the meantime, please allow us to replace your gloves.

Mark Meadows, Customer Service   800-555-0468
Lotus Supports
P.O. Box 390
Dubuque, IA 52001

7. What does Mr. Meadows indicate about the reviewer's issue?
   (A) That it was probably caused by misuse
   (B) That it happens from time to time
   (C) That it can be fixed easily by the user
   (D) That it occurs mostly in right-handed gloves

Ⓐ Ⓑ Ⓒ Ⓓ

8. What assumption of the reviewer's does Mr. Meadows question?

(A) That the gloves were a short-term investment

(B) That the gloves were clearly overused

(C) Why the gloves are cheaper than others

(D) How the gloves are poorly packaged

Ⓐ Ⓑ Ⓒ Ⓓ

9. The word "Keeping" In paragraph 2 line 1 is closest in meaning to

(A) Enjoying

(B) Holding

(C) Maintaining

(D) Possessing

Ⓐ Ⓑ Ⓒ Ⓓ

10. What does Mr. Meadows offer the reviewer?

(A) A discount on other products

(B) A new pair of gloves

(C) A different type of gloves

(D) A refund on the purchase

Ⓐ Ⓑ Ⓒ Ⓓ

11. What must the reviewer do to get something from Mr. Meadows?

(A) Provide personal and purchase information by e-mail

(B) Mail the left glove back to the company address

(C) Phone Mr. Meadows to explain the situation in detail

(D) Send pictures of the defective glove to Mr. Meadows

Ⓐ Ⓑ Ⓒ Ⓓ

TOPICS

第2部
トピック別

- **Unit 7 On the Move**
  交通―バス・電車・飛行機

- **Unit 8 On the Menu/On the Itinerary**
  メニュー・旅行日程―観光・レストラン・ホテル

- **Unit 9 On Sale/On Order**
  販売・注文―ショッピング（直売・オンライン商品）

- **Unit 10 Off the Clock**
  余暇―レジャー・エンターテイメント

- **Unit 11 On the Air**
  放送―メディア・広告

- **Unit 12 On the Agenda**
  議題―会議・スケジュール

- **Unit 13 At the Office**
  オフィス―交渉・販売

- **Unit 14 During the Interview**
  面接―就活・自己 PR

On the Move—Buses, Trains & Planes

交通―バス・電車・飛行機

Parts 1–4 Listening

Sound Advice

Listening の Warm-up から始めましょう。リスニングセクションを解く鍵のひとつは、文章中の2つの単語が連結して発音が変わる現象（いわゆるリエゾン）を聞き取れるようになることです。

これから聞く8つの文章には、her, him, his, it, them のどれかの単語が含まれていますが、最初の部分が前の単語と連結して聞き取れなかったりしています。

● Exercise

🎧 2-02～09

音声を聞き、それぞれの文章に含まれている単語を○で囲んでください。

1. her　him　his　it　them
2. her　him　his　it　them
3. her　him　his　it　them
4. her　him　his　it　them

5. her　him　his　it　them
6. her　him　his　it　them
7. her　him　his　it　them
8. her　him　his　it　them

Vocabulary Warm-up

以下の1から12は輸送・交通に関する語句です。

それぞれの語句に当てはまる交通機関（B, P, T または A）を選んでそのアルファベットを記入してください。正解は1つあるいは2つです。

| B：Buses バス | P：Planes 飛行機 |
| T：Trains 電車 | A：All 上記のすべての交通機関 |

解答例） Jetway* (jet bridge) ___P___　　ticket ___A___　　ticket window ___B, T___

1. waiting area ____
2. to transfer ____
3. to transit ____
4. platform ____

5. stop ____
6. conductor ____
7. pilot ____
8. track ____

9. aisle seat ____
10. driver ____
11. depot ____
12. terminal ____

Part 1　写真描写問題 ···

写真について最も適切なものを選んでください。

🎧 2-10、11

1.

Ⓐ Ⓑ Ⓒ Ⓓ

2.

Ⓐ Ⓑ Ⓒ Ⓓ

General Information

Jetway (jet bridge, boarding bridge)　搭乗ブリッジ

Jetway は固有名詞で、米国内で、空港と航空機の間を結ぶ連絡橋（搭乗ブリッジ）を最も多く生産しているメーカーの名前ですが、搭乗ブリッジそのものを意味する単語としてよく使われています。

Part 2　応答問題

質問の応答として最も適切なものを選んでください。　2-12〜15

1. Mark your answer.　　Ⓐ Ⓑ Ⓒ

2. Mark your answer.　　Ⓐ Ⓑ Ⓒ

3. Mark your answer.　　Ⓐ Ⓑ Ⓒ

4. Mark your answer.　　Ⓐ Ⓑ Ⓒ

Part 3　会話問題

設問の解答として最も適切なものを選んでください。　2-16、17

1. Where is the man at the moment?
(A) At his house in Philadelphia
(B) At the train station in Philadelphia
(C) At the airport in New York
(D) At the bus stop at JFK Airport　　　Ⓐ Ⓑ Ⓒ Ⓓ

2. Why does the woman suggest such an early train?
(A) It is the only train that day.
(B) The airlines suggest arriving two hours prior to take off.
(C) It is a very long ride to New York.
(D) The train station is far from the airport.　　Ⓐ Ⓑ Ⓒ Ⓓ

3. What does the man mean when he says, "That will work"?
(A) He wants the schedule the woman suggests.
(B) He thinks a taxi is better than the train.
(C) He thinks the woman is doing a good job.
(D) He believes the train will leave on time.　　Ⓐ Ⓑ Ⓒ Ⓓ

設問の解答として最も適切なものを選んでください。

 2-18、19

Previous Newbury Bound Schedule

TRAIN	DEPARTURE	PLATFORM
LOCAL	1:51	3
SEMI-EXPRESS	1:57	5
SUPER EXPRESS	2:00	10
REGULAR EXPRESS	2:07	15

1. Where is the announcement being heard?
   (A) Inside the local train
   (B) Inside the semi express train
   (C) Inside the terminal
   (D) Outside of the train station

Ⓐ Ⓑ Ⓒ Ⓓ

2. When does the super express leave?
   (A) In two minutes
   (B) In five minutes
   (C) In ten minutes
   (D) In fifteen minutes

Ⓐ Ⓑ Ⓒ Ⓓ

3. Look at the chart. Which platform number on this old schedule is no longer accurate?
   (A) Platform 3
   (B) Platform 5
   (C) Platform 10
   (D) Platform 15

Ⓐ Ⓑ Ⓒ Ⓓ

Parts 5–7 Reading

Grammar Review

形容詞の使い分け（-ed と -ing）

bored と boring のような -ed と -ing をともなった形容詞の使い分けは英語を母語にしない人たちが間違いやすいポイントの1つです。ただし、この2つの使い分けは規則を抑えれば、それほど混乱を生じることはありません。

● **Analysis 1 -ed**

　　-ed は生き物（人や動物）が持つ感情を表す。

-ed は自分または誰かが直接受けた感情、直接受けた被害を表します。

　例　○　　My son was excited to see the super express.

　　　×　　That super express movie was excited.

● **Analysis 2 -ing**

　-ing は人や物の行動、状況、状態を表します。

　例　○　　I wanted to quit my job because the job was boring.

　　　×　　I was boring watching the same train movie over and over again.

　　*非人称の it で始まる文は必ず -ing 形式の形容詞が用いられる。

-ed か -ing かを選ぶ設問で、"It is (was) _____" の形を目にしたら、下線部に入るのは、-ing 形式の形容詞です。

● Exercise

では実際に -ed／-ing に関する Part 5 問題を2問解いてください。

1. The airlines realize that a long flight can be ------, so they have all improved and expanded their in-flight entertainment selections.

   (A) bored　　　　　　　　(B) boredom

   (C) bore　　　　　　　　 (D) boring　　　　　　　Ⓐ Ⓑ Ⓒ Ⓓ

2. Subway users always get ------ with the unreliable transportation system especially during commuting hours.

   (A) frustrated　　　　　　(B) frustration

   (C) frustrate　　　　　　 (D) frustrating　　　　　Ⓐ Ⓑ Ⓒ Ⓓ

Part 5　短文穴埋め問題 ....

文を完成するのに最も適切なものを選んでください。

1. We regret to announce that the ------ of the 6:55 train to Cedar Rapids will be delayed due to bad weather.
   (A) depart
   (B) departure
   (C) departs
   (D) departed
   (A) (B) (C) (D)

2. There are choices of entrées on all international flights, but those who don't eat meat may request a vegetarian meal ------.
   (A) although
   (B) despite
   (C) whether
   (D) instead
   (A) (B) (C) (D)

3. Trevor ------ dropped his boarding pass after the security checkpoint and had to go the check-in counter to have it reissued.
   (A) gradually
   (B) naturally
   (C) suddenly
   (D) accidentally
   (A) (B) (C) (D)

Part 6　長文穴埋め問題 ....

文を完成するのに最も適切なものを選んでください。

From:　customerservice@transcanair.com

To:　Kenneth Feldman

Date:　November 26

Subject: Recent Flight Survey

Dear Kenneth,

We sent you an email previously ---1.--- your flight from Indianapolis (IND) to Toronto (YYZ) on 6 November, on Trans-Canada Airways, yet we have not heard back from you. We know you have a choice in travel providers, so we appreciate when you choose ---2.--- with us. As a valued CanDoMiles member, your feedback is important and will help us to continue to improve our service. ---3.--- Please begin this short survey **by answering** the first question below: If clicking the number of your response does not take you on to the rest of the survey, you can access it through this URL: https://transcanair.com/flight.service.survey/clickthru

How likely are you to ---- Trans-Canadian Airways to others?
4.

5	4	3	2	1
Definitely Would	- Probably Would	- Might	- Probably Would Not	- Definitely Would Not

We thank you in advance for your time and hope to see you onboard again soon.

Sincerely,
Stephanie Brooks
Chief Operating Officer

1. (A) in addition to
   (B) with regard to
   (C) in place of
   (D) on behalf of
   Ⓐ Ⓑ Ⓒ Ⓓ

2. (A) fly   (B) to fly
   (C) in flight   (D) flew
   Ⓐ Ⓑ Ⓒ Ⓓ

3. (A) We hope we can ask for just a few minutes of your time.
   (B) We have just a few questions about your answers.
   (C) You will be able to find answers on the final screen of the survey.
   (D) You can expect a reply from us in 5-7 business days.
   Ⓐ Ⓑ Ⓒ Ⓓ

4. (A) recognize
   (B) reapply
   (C) recommend
   (D) reconcile
   Ⓐ Ⓑ Ⓒ Ⓓ

設問の解答として最も適切なものを選んでください。

Text-message chain

Neil Epstein [5:50 P.M.]
Just got to the subway exit, but I don't see you…

Rita Salazar [5:51 P.M.]
There are lots of exits. Can you tell which one?

Neil Epstein [5:52 P.M.]
I'm already outside. I can't see a number. There's a fast food place and a coffee shop.

Rita Salazar [5:53 P.M.]
I can't see those, so you are either at the north or west exit. What's the name of the fast food place?

Neil Epstein [5:53 P.M.]
Queen Burger.

Rita Salazar [5:54 P.M.]
Give me a sec. I'll ask someone where it is.

Rita Salazar [5:55 P.M.]
Okay. I got directions. I'm near a newsstand. I'd like to pick up a newspaper first.

Neil Epstein [5:55 P.M.]
Sure, be my guest.

Neil Epstein [5:57 P.M.]
I'm going to cross the street and wait in front Queen Burger.

Rita Salazar [5:57 P.M.]
OK, be there soon.

1. What is suggested about Ms. Salazar and Mr. Epstein?
(A) They are meeting for fast food.
(B) They are stopping for coffee.
(C) They are looking for one another.
(D) They work at a newsstand.

Ⓐ Ⓑ Ⓒ Ⓓ

2. At 5:55, what does Mr. Epstein mean when he writes, "Sure, be my guest"?
(A) He doesn't mind if she stops.
(B) He would like to join her.
(C) He wants her to get him a newspaper.
(D) He wants to buy her lunch.

Ⓐ Ⓑ Ⓒ Ⓓ

On the Menu/On the Itinerary
—Sightseeing, Restaurants & Hotels

メニュー・旅行日程─観光・レストラン・ホテル

Parts 1–4 Listening

Sound Advice

文の前半に集中して聞き取る

Unit 1 の Part 2 で学習したとおり、日本語では文の後半を聞き取るのが大事ですが、英語では文の前半に集中することが必要です。

● Exercise

🎧 2-21〜32

では質問文の最初の単語に集中して聞き取る演習を行います。これから 12 の質問文が流れますので、質問文の最初の単語を聞き取り、以下の空所に書き入れてください。

1. _____	7. _____
2. _____	8. _____
3. _____	9. _____
4. _____	10. _____
5. _____	11. _____
6. _____	12. _____

Vocabulary Warm–up

以下の 1 〜 8 の文章は、メニューや旅行日程に関連があります。
それぞれの空所に当てはまる語句を (A) 〜 (L) の中から選んで、文章を完成してください。

1. If a restaurant brings the food to your house or lets you pick up food and bring it home, they offer _____ and _____.

2. To register at a hotel or resort is to _____, while what you do when you leave is to _____.

3. The course that you begin a meal with is the _____ course.

4. The meaning of _____ and _____ is something that is wrong or miscalculated.

5. If you spend three nights in a hotel, it is a three-night _____.

6. A situation with a long table or tables with large trays of food, usually with all-you-can-eat service, is called a _____.

7. You can buy bread and cookies at a _____. They sometimes even have seats where you can sit and enjoy your _____.

8. People visit _____ to look at various plants and flowers.

(A) appetizer   (G) check out
(B) bakery   (H) error
(C) botanical gardens (I) mistake
(D) buffet   (J) purchase
(E) delivery   (K) stay
(F) check in   (L) take-out

Mini Practice Test

Part 1 写真描写問題

写真について最も適切なものを選んでください。

🎧 2-33、34

1.

Ⓐ Ⓑ Ⓒ Ⓓ

2.

Ⓐ Ⓑ Ⓒ Ⓓ

Part 2　応答問題

質問の応答として最も適切なものを選んでください。

2-35～38

1. Mark your answer.　Ⓐ Ⓑ Ⓒ

2. Mark your answer.　Ⓐ Ⓑ Ⓒ

3. Mark your answer.　Ⓐ Ⓑ Ⓒ

4. Mark your answer.　Ⓐ Ⓑ Ⓒ

Part 3　会話問題

設問の解答として最も適切なものを選んでください。

2-39、40

1. Where most likely is the conversation taking place?
(A) In an art museum
(B) At an office
(C) At a bakery
(D) At a restaurant

Ⓐ Ⓑ Ⓒ Ⓓ

2. Why does the man say "You should take a peek before I pack up the box"?
(A) He does not want the woman to tear the box.
(B) He needs the woman to check for errors.
(C) He wants the woman to admire the cake.
(D) He wants the woman to agree to buy it.

Ⓐ Ⓑ Ⓒ Ⓓ

3. What does the man promise to do?
(A) Introduce the woman to the baker
(B) Make a brand new one
(C) Take care of the mistake
(D) Give it to the woman for free

Ⓐ Ⓑ Ⓒ Ⓓ

Part 4　説明文問題 ••

設問の解答として最も適切なものを選んでください。

 2-41、42

Contribution Log for Tuesday Evening, September 15

Name	Tour Time	Donation
Damian Brock	5:20	$15
Linda Yamamoto	6:00	$25
Marilyn Pearson	8:40	$10
Alexander Martinez	9:00	$12

1. Why does the museum now have special hours?
   (A) Because the season has recently changed.
   (B) Because it has been recently remodeled.
   (C) Because it has received extra contributions.
   (D) Because of the busy tour schedule.

   Ⓐ Ⓑ Ⓒ Ⓓ

2. Look at the graphic. Which contributor was most likely to have listened to the announcement?
   (A) Mr. Brock
   (B) Ms. Yamamoto
   (C) Ms. Pearson
   (D) Mr. Martinez

   Ⓐ Ⓑ Ⓒ Ⓓ

3. How does the gift shop support the museum?
   (A) All of the profits go to the museum.
   (B) Ten percent of the purchase price goes to the museum.
   (C) There is a donation box on the counter.
   (D) The museum receives about a third of the purchase price.

   Ⓐ Ⓑ Ⓒ Ⓓ

Grammar Review

似ていて間違えやすい前置詞

　似たような働きをする前置詞の使い分けは、英語を母語としない学習者にとって難関のひとつです。ただ暗記するのではなく、前置詞のもつ役割・特性を把握することが大切です。

at と **in** と **on**

（場所）at は「特定の場所を点の感覚でとらえた場合」、in は「広い場所や周りに境界線のある場所に」、on は「表面や線上の位置」を表し、壁にかけてあったり天井にくっついている場合にも用います。

　例）He is **at** the bus stop.

　　　He is **in** the dining room.

　　　There is a spider **on** the ceiling.

（時）at は限られた時点、in は月、季節、年など 1 日よりも長い時間、on は 1 日だけを表します。

　例）I saw him **at** midnight.

　　　He was born **in** 1957.

　　　We went to that hotel **on** Friday.

after と **in** （時間）

どちらも「後」を意味しますが、after は過去のことを、in は未来のことを表します。

　例）I wasn't going to ask her to help, but I finally called her **after** three days.

　　　I will call her again **in** three days.

for と **to** （目的）

for は出発点を基準に目的へ「向かう」ことに、to は到達点を基準に目的に「到達する」ことに重点が置かれます。

　例）I left **for** Honolulu at 8 P.M.

　　　※ホノルルに向かって出発したことが重点で実際に到達したかは重要ではない。

　　　He went **to** Honolulu at 8 P.M.

　　　※ホノルルに到達したことが重点。

by と **until**（時間）

　by はある時間まで（＝その時間より遅くならない）ときに、until は動作状態がある時間までずっと続く（＝その時に動作状態が終わる）ときに用います。

　例）I have to check out of this hotel **by** 11:00 A.M.

　　　I can stay at the hotel **until** 11:00 A.M.

● **Exercise**

1 〜 4 の文の空所に当てはまる前置詞を (A) 〜 (H) から選んでください。

1. I'll let you know what I decide _____ a few weeks.
2. Could you help me put the poster _____ the wall?
3. We don't need to leave _____ the airport _____ 9:30.
4. The professor asked us to finish the report _____ Tuesday.

(A) after　　(B) at　　(C) by　　(D) for　　(E) in　　(F) on　　(G) to　　(H) until

Mini Practice Test

Part 5　文法問題 ・・・

文を完成するのに最も適切な選択肢を選んでください。

1. Since it was located so close to the ocean, we were surprised that the restaurant didn't put any fish ------- their soups or stews.

(A) at
(B) in
(C) on
(D) with

Ⓐ Ⓑ Ⓒ Ⓓ

2. At that hotel, if you don't call ahead or check in ------- 6 P.M., they may end up giving your room away.

(A) by
(B) for
(C) since
(D) until

Ⓐ Ⓑ Ⓒ Ⓓ

3. If you plan to stay ------- more than a night, you might want to look at packaged tours.

(A) until
(B) for
(C) after
(D) to

Ⓐ Ⓑ Ⓒ Ⓓ

文を完成させるのに最も適切なものを選んでください。

To our valued guests

Thank you for choosing the **Royal Crest Lodge**. We know there are numerous places to stay in the area, so we would like to offer you a small ---1.--- of our appreciation. As our gift to you, you may either ---2.--- a free day pass to our deluxe gym or a 2-hour morning spa session (8 A.M.-12 P.M.). Please contact the concierge at extension 220 to make ---3.--- . Also, you will find complimentary bottled water and a fruit plate in your refrigerator. If there is anything else we can do to make your stay more comfortable, please do not hesitate to contact us. ---4.---

1. (A) label   (B) token
    (C) mark   (D) point

                                             Ⓐ Ⓑ Ⓒ Ⓓ

2. (A) choice   (B) choose
    (C) chose   (D) chosen

                                             Ⓐ Ⓑ Ⓒ Ⓓ

3. (A) arrangements
    (B) assignments
    (C) associations
    (D) attachments

                                             Ⓐ Ⓑ Ⓒ Ⓓ

4. (A) We are happy that you are comfortable.
    (B) We hope you enjoy your stay.
    (C) We will send you information about our sister hotels.
    (D) We hope you like the spa service.

                                             Ⓐ Ⓑ Ⓒ Ⓓ

設問の解答として最も適切なものを選んでください。

Advertisement

Crystal Lake Resort and Country Club
One resort, so many choices!

Located just outside of Orlando, a hop, skip and a jump from Florida's biggest attractions, Crystal Lake is the perfect setting for a magical vacation experience you'll always remember. Relax and enjoy the lush 1200-acre landscape and luxurious accommodations—from fully equipped one-, two- and three-bedroom villas to comfortable, convenient motel suites. Choose from an amazing variety of amenities and activities. While you'll be close to the action, you can find something for everyone without ever leaving the resort!

From $79 per night for a motel suite (1-2 persons)
To $199 per night for a 3-bedroom, 2-bath villa (3-6 persons)

At Crystal Lake, you'll find:
- -The Legends at Crystal Lake—18 holes of championship golf.
- -Legends Walk—a 9-hole, par 3 walking course lit for nighttime play.
- -The Crystal Course—18 challenging holes of golf.
- -Family-oriented Pink Flamingo—a 9-hole, mini-golf course

Plus
An amazing variety of pools and spas, court sports, restaurants, shops, arcades, playgrounds, and more!

Coupon

Save big at Crystal Lake Resort.
Choose the discount system that is best for you:

A. 5% THIS COUPON

Show this coupon! (May be combined with other discounts)

B. 10% **FLORIDA** RESIDENT DISCOUNT (May be combined with other discounts)

Show your **FL** driver's license or State ID.

C. 20% SENIOR DISCOUNT (May **NOT** be combined with other discounts)

For individuals/groups accompanying person(s) age 65+

D. 25% LONG STAY (May **NOT** be combined with other discounts)

For stays of <u>five</u> consecutive nights or more.

Call: 888-555-1700

Or e-mail reservations@cryslakfl.com with your phone number and we will contact you.

Crystal Lake Resort Super Coupon Book

E-mail

To: reservations@cryslakfl.com

From: jbarstow@fl.yy.net

Subject: Reservations

To whom it may concern:

I saw your coupon on page 17 of the Super Coupon Book. I would like to reserve one of your largest villas for a group of five—my 75-year-old mother, my two children, my husband and myself. We would check in late in the afternoon on May 6 and check out the morning of May 10. We will be coming from our home in Palm Beach that morning and should arrive at around 3 P.M.

Could you please figure out the best discount for us and then be in touch with me in the way that you mention on the coupon? We are excited about being able to get to all the Crystal Lake Resort activities so easily!

Sincerely,

Jill

Jill Barstow (and family)

345 Pelican Ln.

Palm Beach, FL 33480

Cell: 561-555-8052

1. Why most likely is this resort successful?
   (A) There are few places to stay nearby.
   (B) It holds a golf championship every year.
   (C) There are playgrounds on the property.
   (D) It is close to many popular attractions.

   Ⓐ Ⓑ Ⓒ Ⓓ

2. How should the person reading the e-mail get in touch with Ms. Barstow?
   (A) E-mail Ms. Barstow back
   (B) Wait for her phone call
   (C) Write a confirmation letter to her
   (D) Call her on the phone

   Ⓐ Ⓑ Ⓒ Ⓓ

3. What kind of accommodation does Ms. Barstow wish to book?
   (A) A motel suite   (B) A one-bedroom villa
   (C) A two-bedroom villa   (D) A three-bedroom villa

   Ⓐ Ⓑ Ⓒ Ⓓ

4. In paragraph 2, line 1 of the e-mail, the expression "figure out" is closest in meaning to:
   (A) solve   (B) determine
   (C) add   (D) commence

   Ⓐ Ⓑ Ⓒ Ⓓ

5. Which is the best deal that can be applied to the Barstow group?
   (A) The RESIDENT discount
   (B) The COUPON + RESIDENT discounts
   (C) The SENIOR discount
   (D) The LONG STAY discount

   Ⓐ Ⓑ Ⓒ Ⓓ

On Sale/On Order—Shopping
(Bricks & Mortar, Online Goods & Supplies)

販売・注文—ショッピング（直売・オンライン商品）

Parts 1–4 Listening

Sound Advice

カタカナ英語に引きずられない！

　海外から言葉を取り入れた「外来語」はカタカナで表記されることがほとんどです。日本で何の気なしに使っているその単語は、ネイティブの発音と全く異なることがあり、このことは日本人が英語を聞き取る際に大きな障害となります。

　たとえばhot（暑い・熱い）は外来語としてホットの発音で日常的に使われています。しかしながら、大多数の英語のネイティブはこの単語を /hɑt/ と発音します。

● Exercise

CD 2-44、45

まずすべての発音をしっかり聞いてください。次に1〜8の単語が、それぞれ A、B、C のどの単語のものかを聞き取り、最も適切なものを1つ選んでください。

	A	B	C
1.	bot	bought	boat
2.	cot	caught	coat
3.	dot	---	dote
4.	got	---	goat
5.	not	naught	note
6.	rot	wrought	rote
7.	sot	sought	---
8.	tot	taught	tote

Vocabulary Warm-up

1〜5の語句はいずれも COST(価格) に関連したものです。知らない語句がある場合は最大限に推量を働かせ、"expensive" を意味するものには「↑」を、"inexpensive" を意味するものには「↓」を語句の後に書き入れてください。

1. a pretty penny ＿＿＿
2. quite reasonable ＿＿＿
3. rather extravagant ＿＿＿
4. a bit steep ＿＿＿
5. for a song ＿＿＿

Mini Practice Test

写真について最も適切なものを選んでください。

CD 2-46、47

1.

Ⓐ Ⓑ Ⓒ Ⓓ

2.

Ⓐ Ⓑ Ⓒ Ⓓ

質問の応答として最も適切なものを選んでください。

 2-48〜51

1. Mark your answer.　　Ⓐ Ⓑ Ⓒ

2. Mark your answer.　　Ⓐ Ⓑ Ⓒ

3. Mark your answer.　　Ⓐ Ⓑ Ⓒ

4. Mark your answer.　　Ⓐ Ⓑ Ⓒ

....

設問の解答として最も適切なものを選んでください。 2-52、53

1. Who is the woman?
   (A) A shop clerk
   (B) A baker
   (C) A customer
   (D) The manager

   Ⓐ　Ⓑ　Ⓒ　Ⓓ

2. Why is the woman having trouble locating the item?
   (A) She is not looking in the right place.
   (B) The customer service counter put her on hold.
   (C) The store does not have it in stock at the moment.
   (D) They moved the item to another place in the store.

   Ⓐ　Ⓑ　Ⓒ　Ⓓ

3. What will the woman most likely do?
   (A) Get the lower price at a later date
   (B) Buy the item today at a special price
   (C) Pre-order the item through the manager
   (D) Buy the item at another store

   Ⓐ　Ⓑ　Ⓒ　Ⓓ

Part 4　説明文問題 ....

設問の解答として最も適切なものを選んでください。 2-54、55

1. What is the main point of the announcement?
   (A) To welcome shoppers to the store
   (B) To get new members for their club
   (C) To advertise some special sales
   (D) To let people know they are closing

   Ⓐ　Ⓑ　Ⓒ　Ⓓ

2. For which items does the speaker mention a specific discount?

    (A) Children's clothing

    (B) Kitchen goods

    (C) Men's suits

    (D) Suitcases

Ⓐ Ⓑ Ⓒ Ⓓ

3. What does the announcer imply about the store closing?

    (A) That it will be happening soon

    (B) That people need to check out

    (C) That it is later than usual

    (D) That shoppers should take their time

Ⓐ Ⓑ Ⓒ Ⓓ

Parts 5–7 Reading

Grammar Review

間違えやすい副詞 — almost, almost all, most —

almost の意味

almost は「何かに到達する一歩手前」という意味を持ちます。

    I **almost** finished my homework.

    It's **almost** ten o'clock.

almost は名詞と一緒には使えない

「ほとんどの人」のように量や程度を表したい場合、「almost（副詞）＋名詞」は、文法的に間違いです。almost の後には all などの程度・量を表す形容詞が必要です。

    × **Almost** Japanese people make this mistake.

    ○ **Almost** all Japanese people make this mistake.

「ほとんど〜ある」場合と「ほとんど〜ない」場合で almost に続く言葉が変わります。

        「ほとんど〜ある」all, every, always など

    例）He **almost always** stops by that store after school.

        「ほとんど〜ない」 no, none, nothing, never など

    例）**Almost nobody** was there.

most と most of の違い

どちらも「ほとんどの〜（名詞）」という言い方をする場合に使いますが、most は一般的な対象に、most of は特定の対象に使います。

例） **Most** products can be ordered online.

例） **Most of** our company's products can be ordered online.

● Exercise

1〜4の文の空所に当てはまる語句を (A) 〜 (D) から選んでください。（正解は2つの場合もあります。）

1. He doesn't know much about sneakers, so he needed to rely _____ on his friend.
2. _____ her friends know the first day of every month is a special sale day at the supermarket.
3. When our phone rings at dinner time at home, it is _____ a sales call.
4. If you're _____ finished with your shopping, you can take a break and have some snacks.

(A) almost　　(B) almost entirely　　(C) almost always　　(D) most of

Mini Practice Test

Part 5　文法問題

文を完成するのに最も適切なものを選んでください。

1. I was going to order some coffee until I realized that ------- my colleagues who drink coffee had already left the office.
   (A) almost
   (B) almost all of
   (C) almost always
   (D) almost entirely

Ⓐ Ⓑ Ⓒ Ⓓ

2. ------- Joe's friends bought new computers when they got to college, but he already had one that had been a high school graduation present.
(A) Almost
(B) Most of
(C) Almost of
(D) Most of all

Ⓐ Ⓑ Ⓒ Ⓓ

3. These days, Cynthia gets ------- things online, but she does still like to shop downtown on the weekends and when she's got some time off.
(A) most
(B) almost
(C) most of
(D) almost always

Ⓐ Ⓑ Ⓒ Ⓓ

Part 6 長文穴埋め問題

文を完成するのに最も適切なものを選んでください。

Book Emporium going-out-of-business sale, April 18
We would like to thank all of our loyal customers for your business over the past 35 years. As one of the last bookstores in the city, we are sad to shutter our doors. Our father ---1.--- this business toward the end of the twentieth century at the height of the bookstore café era. Not only did Book Emporium have the latest books and magazines, but it won Best Coffee in Cedarville three years in a row in the 90s. ---2.---
As everyone is well aware, ---3.--- buys their books and magazines in person these days. We held on as long as we could through these changes in society. We even considered becoming a full-fledged café, but we realized that would ---4.--- a completely different business model and level of expertise that we were not equipped to handle.
We would like to invite you all to our final sale. All items, including bookshelves, chairs, etc. will be available for a song. Expect discounts of up to 90%. On April 18, doors open at 10 A.M. and close either at 10 P.M. or when we've sold everything but the front door.

1. (A) began   (B) begun
   (C) has begun   (D) was beginning

   Ⓐ Ⓑ Ⓒ Ⓓ

2. (A) That is to say we also had a big collection of books on coffee.
   (B) For that reason the store was located in the tallest building on the block.
   (C) Needless to say many coffee lovers will also be sorry to see us go.
   (D) That is why our father always ordered many copies of that magazine.

   Ⓐ Ⓑ Ⓒ Ⓓ

3. (A) most nobody   (B) almost nobody
   (C) anybody else   (D) most anybody

   Ⓐ Ⓑ Ⓒ Ⓓ

4. (A) remain   (B) receive
   (C) require   (D) replace

   Ⓐ Ⓑ Ⓒ Ⓓ

Part 7   読解問題

設問の解答として最も適切なものを選んでください。

Advertisement

Crawford's Department Store

Just-in-time gift sale
Gifts for her, for him, for you!
Open extra hours throughout the holiday season

From 7 A.M. to 11 P.M.
Seven days a week

25% off all sleepwear	Reg. $18-$98	Sale $13.5-$73.50
50% off women's sweaters	Reg. $40-$68	Sale $20.0-$34.00
30% off fashion jewelry	Reg. $14-$55	Sale $ 9.8-$38.50
SALE leather boat shoes	$49.99	Reg. $69.00
SALE roasting pan	$29.99	Reg. $59.99
SALE 12-cup coffee maker	$99.99	Reg. $109.99

1. How much is the savings on pajamas?
(A) 25%
(B) $80
(C) About $5
(D) $13.50-$73.50   Ⓐ Ⓑ Ⓒ Ⓓ

2. In which department would you find the most expensive items?
(A) Women's fashion
(B) Footwear
(C) Jewelry
(D) Housewares   Ⓐ Ⓑ Ⓒ Ⓓ

3. What is special about their holiday hours?
(A) They are open 12 hours a day.
(B) They are open seven days a week.
(C) They are open longer.
(D) They are open Monday through Friday.   Ⓐ Ⓑ Ⓒ Ⓓ

Unit 10

Off the Clock —Leisure & Entertainment

余暇—レジャー・エンターテイメント

Parts 1–4 Listening

Sound Advice

can と can't の聞き分け

can と can't はどちらも /kin/ のように聞こえて、聞き分けが難しいです。これは、/t/ と /n/ の 2 つの音は口の中の同じ部分を使って発音されるため、いくらか鼻音化され、/t/ がはっきり聞こえず、どちらも /kin/ のように聞こえるからです。

聞き分けのポイントはストレス（stress＝ 強調）

ほとんどの場合、文の中で can't は強調して発音しますが、can は強調されることはありません。例外は、相手から能力を問われて、反論「できることを強調」する場合です。

You **can't** reach that box.

Yes, I **can**.

同じように「できることを強調」する文章で can を使う場合でも、can が文章の真ん中あたりで使われる場合には、can は強調されず、むしろ、/kn/ と弱いアクセントで発音されます。

例）I'm sure I **can** do it.

● Exercise

 2-57〜62

次の 1 〜 6 の英文を聞き、それぞれ can と can't のどちらの発音がされているのかを判断し、正しいものに〇をつけてください。

1. can   can't
2. can   can't
3. can   can't
4. can   can't
5. can   can't
6. can   can't

96

Vocabulary Warm-up

②〜⑦の ACTIVITY につながりのある単語を、以下の例のように、WORDS 1 と WORDS 2 から選んでください。　　**例　①- G -3**

それぞれの ACTIVITY につながりのある単語は WORDS 1 にも WORDS 2 にも複数ありますが、ACTIVITY-WORDS 1 -WORDS 2 のつながりとして最適なものを考えてみてください。

ACTIVITY	RELATED WORDS 1	RELATED WORDS 2
① ballet	A. kick	1. deck
② hiking	B. deal	2. hoop
③ soccer	C. skate	3. slippers
④ basketball	D. dribble	4. goal
⑤ hockey	E. sing	5. performer
⑥ concert	F. walk	6. boots
⑦ cards	G. dance	7. ice

② – (　　　) – (　　　)　　⑤ – (　　　) – (　　　)

③ – (　　　) – (　　　)　　⑥ – (　　　) – (　　　)

④ – (　　　) – (　　　)　　⑦ – (　　　) – (　　　)

Mini Practice Test

Part 1　写真描写問題 ······································

写真について最も適切なものを選んでください。

🎧 2-63、64

1.

Ⓐ Ⓑ Ⓒ Ⓓ

2.

Ⓐ Ⓑ Ⓒ Ⓓ

....

質問の応答として最も適切なものを選んでください。 2-65〜68

　1. Mark your answer.　　(A) (B) (C)

　2. Mark your answer.　　(A) (B) (C)

　3. Mark your answer.　　(A) (B) (C)

　4. Mark your answer.　　(A) (B) (C)

Part 3　会話問題 ....

設問の応答として最も適切なものを選んでください。 2-69、70

　1. Where does this conversation most likely take place?
　　(A) At a stable
　　(B) On a racetrack
　　(C) In a vet's office
　　(D) At the zoo

(A) (B) (C) (D)

　2. Why does the man say, "keep it up"?
　　(A) To encourage the woman to stay calm
　　(B) To have the woman move the saddle
　　(C) To get the woman to face forward
　　(D) To ask the woman for her help

(A) (B) (C) (D)

　3. What does the man offer to do?
　　(A) Calm down the horse for her
　　(B) Assist her in adjusting the saddle
　　(C) Help her by riding along with her
　　(D) Take the saddle off the horse

(A) (B) (C) (D)

Part 4　説明文問題 ....

設問の応答として最も適切なものを選んでください。

🔊 2-71、72

Lake Martin Attractions

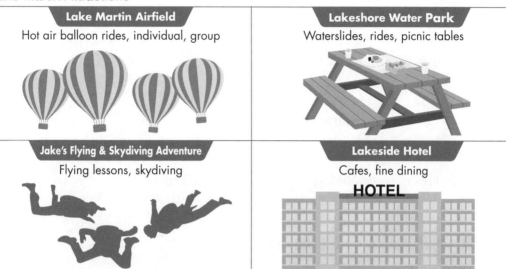

1. What was being celebrated last weekend?
   (A) The speaker's 30th anniversary
   (B) 25 years of marriage
   (C) A family reunion
   (D) A cousin's wedding

   Ⓐ Ⓑ Ⓒ Ⓓ

2. How many events did the family enjoy on the weekend?
   (A) Almost 50
   (B) Three, one on Saturday and two on Sunday
   (C) Three, two on Saturday and one on Sunday
   (D) Eight times

   Ⓐ Ⓑ Ⓒ Ⓓ

3. Look at the graphic. What activity does the speaker mention taking place on the last day?
   (A) A hot air balloon ride
   (B) Skydiving lessons at Jake's
   (C) A picnic lunch at the water park
   (D) Lunch at a nice restaurant

   Ⓐ Ⓑ Ⓒ Ⓓ

Parts 5–7 Reading

Grammar Review

●不定詞と動名詞の使い分け Infinitives/Gerunds

不定詞は「潜在的あるいは未来の出来事」に、動名詞は「今現在起きている行動あるいはすでに実行された行動」に用いられます。

使い分けの基本ルール

1. 不定詞　He wants **to learn** Spanish.
　　　　　　→将来習うつもりがあるがまだ実現していない。

2. 動名詞　He enjoys **speaking** Spanish with his friends.
　　　　　　→彼は既にスペイン語で話す経験を積んでいる。

●同一動詞で、不定詞と動名詞で意味が違う場合

1. （不定詞）　He **stopped to** talk to his friend
　　　　　　　→これから話しをする。
　　　（動名詞）He **stopped talking** to his friend.
　　　　　　　→今まで話していた。
2. （不定詞）　I **tried to** leave her an e-mail message.
　　　　　　　→メッセージは完了していない。
　　　（動名詞）I **tried leaving** her an e-mail message.
　　　　　　　→メッセージは完了した。

● Exercise

では不定詞と動名詞についての問題を解いてください。

1-5 の文に、それぞれの動詞を正しい形で記入してください。

記入例　(X-ing, to-X, X-ing or to-X)

1. (remember)
   I tried _____ the password to my old account, but nothing I typed in worked.

2. (e-mail)
   Jon and Chris had a big argument and they stopped _____ each other.

3. (travel)
   Before she had children, Nancy really enjoyed _____ .

4. (study)

   We decided _____ Spanish before we got to Mexico so that we could communicate better with the local people.

5. (look)

   Before the job started, Kevin imagined _____ at the street from the window of his big office on the 23rd floor.

Mini Practice Test

Part 5　文法問題 ·

文を完成するのに最も適切な選択肢を選んでください。

1. In spite of reading a positive review, I found the movie so boring that I decided ------ the theater in the middle.
   (A) to leave   (B) leaving
   (C) leave   (D) left

   Ⓐ Ⓑ Ⓒ Ⓓ

2. I enjoy ------ a walk to the park near my house whenever I have some free time.
   (A) take   (B) taking
   (C) to have taken   (D) to take

   Ⓐ Ⓑ Ⓒ Ⓓ

3. I saw a perfect SUV in the showroom, but I can't afford ------ a new one right now.
   (A) bought   (B) buy
   (C) buying   (D) to buy

   Ⓐ Ⓑ Ⓒ Ⓓ

文を完成するのに最も適切なものを選んでください。

August 15

The Middleton Youth Jazz Band ----1.---- their first concert of the season on September 25. There will be eight concerts this year. The tickets are $10 at the door, but season passes good for all performances are only $65. If you purchase your season pass in advance, before September 15, you can get them for the ----2.---- low price of $40! ----3.----, it is a good idea to get yours in the next month. Go online to middletonYJ.com/passes to buy your passes or get them from a band member. This looks to be the best season ever, especially at the end. ----4.----

1. (A) performed
   (B) performing
   (C) will be performing
   (D) will have performed

   Ⓐ Ⓑ Ⓒ Ⓓ

2. (A) immeasurably
   (B) immediately
   (C) incredibly
   (D) inevitably

   Ⓐ Ⓑ Ⓒ Ⓓ

3. (A) Because
   (B) Instead
   (C) Therefore
   (D) Unless

   Ⓐ Ⓑ Ⓒ Ⓓ

4. (A) Be advised that season passes are valid for one season only.
   (B) Suffice it to say all major credit cards are accepted on the website.
   (C) The last concert features a fabulous classic jazz retrospective.
   (D) The pass, of course, entitles you to attend all eight performances.

   Ⓐ Ⓑ Ⓒ Ⓓ

設問の解答として最も適切なものを選んでください。

Offer

An incredible Thanksgiving offer is available for both first-time hang gliders or those with a bit more experience. On Thanksgiving Day, come in to Napa Valley Hang Gliding Adventures and ride for free! This incredible giveaway is the company's way of giving thanks to the community for nearly five years of support.

Hang Gliding Adventures provides tandem (instructor and student together) hang gliding instruction, solo flight rentals, and hang gliding equipment sales and service. The company's goal is to offer quality instruction, service and advice, so that many may experience the purest, most enjoyable form of flight.

Whether you are looking for the quiet, surreal experience of powerless flight, want to go up mid-afternoon and hang out with the birds, or love the roller coasters and are looking for a thrill, Hang Gliding Adventures can give you the experience you seek.

In order to take your free flight on Thanksgiving Day (11/26) call (627) 555-1339 and reserve now!

E-mail 1

To: customerservice@Napahangadv.com
From: Ghidalgo@az.jj.net
Subject: Rain check
Date: June 8

Hi
My name is George Hidalgo. I came in last year on November 23 and enjoyed a paid tandem flight. I was so excited that I also signed up for a free solo flight for your 5th Anniversary on Thanksgiving. As you recall, the weather was really bad that day. When I came for the flight, I was given a raincheck that I was told was good for six months. Unfortunately, I live in Arizona and I left Napa that Friday and have not been back. I just found out that I can be in Napa next week for a few days. My raincheck expired about two weeks ago. I am writing to see if you would consider honoring the rain check for me. In all likelihood, I will book a second solo flight for later in my trip if you can see your way clear to do for me.

I look forward to hearing from you.
George
George B. Hidalgo

E-mail 2

To: Ghidalgo@az.jj.net
From: customerservice@Napahangadv.com
Subject: your rain check
Date: June 10

Dear Mr. Hidalgo,

Thank you for contacting us.
As long as there is an opening in our schedule and you redeem this flight
by the end of this month, we are happy to honor your rain check. I looked
up your account in the computer and found the tandem flight that you
mentioned. Two months ago, there was an article about us on a website
that features Napa activities. Since that time, our bookings have increased
about 40%. The reason I mention this is that you should probably book
both the free flight and the one you were interested in taking toward the
end of your trip as soon as possible.

Kind regards,

Harvey Lowenthal
Senior Manager
Napa Valley Hang Gliding Adventures

1. When did the company most likely start operations?
   (A) About six months before the notice
   (B) Around five and a half years ago
   (C) On Thanksgiving of the previous year
   (D) Exactly one year before the promotion

2. What was necessary to do to take advantage of the company's offer?

(A) Sign up for lessons

(B) Pay for one of their services

(C) Recommend them to a friend

(D) Make a reservation

Ⓐ Ⓑ Ⓒ Ⓓ

3. In the e-mail 1, the word "good" in paragraph 1, line 5, is closest in meaning to

(A) positive

(B) talented

(C) valid

(D) moral

Ⓐ Ⓑ Ⓒ Ⓓ

4. What does Mr. Hidalgo indicate about the Thanksgiving promotion?

(A) The rules about how to claim it were hard to understand.

(B) The weather made it impossible for him to redeem it.

(C) He was not able to get there on Thanksgiving Day.

(D) They insisted he take a lesson before receiving the gift.

Ⓐ Ⓑ Ⓒ Ⓓ

5. What will Mr. Hidalgo most likely do?

(A) Complain to the company about the poor service.

(B) Take a solo flight on his next visit to Napa.

(C) Buy his own hang gliding equipment.

(D) Approach a manager and explain his situation.

Ⓐ Ⓑ Ⓒ Ⓓ

Unit 11

On the Air ―Media & Advertising

放送―メディア・広告

Parts 1–4 Listening

Sound Advice

同じスペリングでも、ストレス（強調）される位置によって用法や意味が違う単語

英語を学習している私たちにとって、ストレス（強調）の習得は文字通りのストレスです。1つの単語を覚えても、その単語が文章の中でストレスされる位置（強調される位置）が違うと、違う単語のように聞こえたりすることがあるので注意が必要です。

品詞によるストレスの位置の違い

名詞 Nouns	動詞 Verbs または形容詞 Adjectives
CONflict (n)　不一致、葛藤	conFLICT (v)　対立する、矛盾する
CONtent (n)　内容、容量	conTENT (v)　～を満足させる (adj)　満足して
DEsert (n)　砂漠	deSERT (v)　～から逃れる、 ～を見捨てる
DIgest (n)　要約	diGEST (v)　消化する
PRODuce (n)　（野菜や果物の）農作物	proDUCE (V)　生産する
PROject (n)　計画、事業	proJECT (v)　突出する、投影する
REFuse (n)　廃棄物	reFUSE (v)　拒否する
SUBject (n)　主題	subJECT (v)　服従させる

Exercise

 2-74～80

1～7の短い英文を聞き、それぞれの単語がAかBのどちらにストレス（強調）が置かれているかを聞き取り、正しい方を選んでください。

	A	B
1. content	CONtent	conTENT
2. desert	Desert	deSERT
3. digest	Digest	diGEST
4. produce	PRODuce	proDUCE
5. project	PROJect	proJECT
6. refuse	REFuse	reFUSE
7. subject	SUBject	subJECT

Vocabulary Warm-up

インタビューでよく用いられる表現

次の1～5の表現は、インタビューによく用いられます。それぞれの応答として最も適している
ものをA～Eの中から選び、その記号を（　　）の中に記してください。

1. What do you do?　　　　　　　　（　　）
2. What do you produce?　　　　　（　　）
3. Perdon me?　　　　　　　　　　（　　）
4. I'm sorry.　　　　　　　　　　　（　　）
5. How can we prevent accidents?　（　　）

| A. Don't worry about it. |
| B. Nothing. I was talking to myself. |
| C. I'm a TV producer. |
| D. By being careful. |
| E. We make films. |

Mini Practice Test

Part 1 　写真描写問題

写真について適切なものを選んでください。

 2-81、82

1.

Ⓐ Ⓑ Ⓒ Ⓓ

2.

Ⓐ Ⓑ Ⓒ Ⓓ

Part 2　応答問題

質問の応答として最も適切なものを選んでください。

 2-83〜86

1. Mark your answer.　Ⓐ Ⓑ Ⓒ

2. Mark your answer.　Ⓐ Ⓑ Ⓒ

3. Mark your answer.　Ⓐ Ⓑ Ⓒ

4. Mark your answer.　Ⓐ Ⓑ Ⓒ

Part 3　会話問題

設問の応答として最も適切なものを選んでください。

 2-87、88

1. Where is this conversation most likely taking place?
   (A) At a movie theater
   (B) In a business meeting
   (C) At a television studio
   (D) In a weather balloon

Ⓐ Ⓑ Ⓒ Ⓓ

2. Why does the man ask about commuting hours?
   (A) To understand the woman's work schedule
   (B) To find out when the weather will change
   (C) To make plans to go to work together
   (D) To figure out what time he needs for work

Ⓐ Ⓑ Ⓒ Ⓓ

3. What advice does the woman give?
   (A) People listening should take a shower tomorrow.
   (B) People listening should not leave the house tomorrow.
   (C) People listening should wear a heavy jacket tomorrow.
   (D) People listening should carry an umbrella tomorrow.

Ⓐ Ⓑ Ⓒ Ⓓ

Part 4　説明文問題

設問の解答として最も適切なものを選んでください。

 2-89、90

East side of the street map

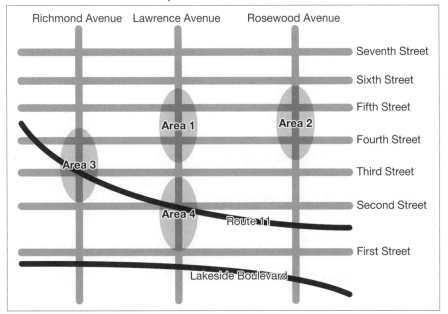

1. Look at the map. Which area is partially closed due to road repair?

   (A) Area 1　　　　　　　(B) Area 2

   (C) Area 3　　　　　　　(D) Area 4　　　　　　Ⓐ Ⓑ Ⓒ Ⓓ

2. What is the situation with traffic on Lakeside Boulevard?

   (A) Traffic there is light as usual.

   (B) The flow of traffic will improve soon.

   (C) A driver has caused some traffic issues.

   (D) One lane of Lakeside Boulevard is closed.　　Ⓐ Ⓑ Ⓒ Ⓓ

3. When is it possible to hear another traffic report?

   (A) In two hours from now

   (B) In ninety minutes

   (C) At 4:00 P.M.

   (D) At 7:00 this evening　　Ⓐ Ⓑ Ⓒ Ⓓ

Grammar Review

間違えやすい接続詞と前置詞
―空所の後ろが節なら接続詞、句ならば前置詞―

while と **during** と **for**　〜の間
while 接続詞
　例）He attended an acting seminar **while** he worked to support us in L.A.
during 前置詞
　例）The phone always seems to ring **during** dinner time.
for 前置詞
　例）We have been reviewing the scenario **for** many weeks.

although と **despite**　〜にもかかわらず
although 接続詞
　例）I like him, **although** I don't trust him.
despite 前置詞
　例）**Despite** his unfriendly manner, he is trusted by everyone.

unless と **except**　〜でなければ／〜以外は
unless 接続詞
　例）My grandfather hardly turns on the TV **unless** he really wants to watch something.
except 前置詞
　例）He doesn't do anything **except** play golf.

● Exercise

1～6の下線部に当てはまる単語を下の（A）～（G）の中から選んで、その記号を書き入れてください。

1. We had lunch _____ we were waiting to go on stage.

2. I don't like this new anchorperson very much, _____ a lot of older people sing his praises.

3. _____ you work all night, you won't be able to finish the project.

4. _____ the fact that it's freezing cold out, Jack is walking around in just a T-shirt.

5. You'll miss your train _____ you hurry.

(A) while   (B) during   (C) for   (D) despite   (E) although   (F) unless   (G) except

Mini Practice Test

Part 5   文法問題

文を完成するのに最も適切な選択肢を選んでください。

1. I'm not planning to go to the meeting ------ Bob is going to be there to explain the new project to us.
(A) except   (B) while
(C) unless   (D) without   Ⓐ Ⓑ Ⓒ Ⓓ

2. She is really hungry, because she did some shopping ------ the lunch hour and she never got a chance to eat lunch.
(A) while   (B) during
(C) about   (D) between   Ⓐ Ⓑ Ⓒ Ⓓ

3. I was told that the new detective drama with all the big-name stars is going to be canceled after one season, ------ it may only be a rumor.
(A) unless   (B) although
(C) until   (D) despite   Ⓐ Ⓑ Ⓒ Ⓓ

文を完成するのに最も適切なものを選んでください。

----1---- As of November 1, Deep South Airways will no longer fly directly from Atlanta to Miami. Furthermore, Atlanta-Memphis flights will be eliminated as of July 31.

However, our Atlanta-Orlando service is now hourly, so passengers may ----2---- from there to our partner, All-Florida Airlines, which has quick flights from Orlando (MCO) to Miami, Tampa, and other cities in Florida, along with longer distances to other US and Caribbean destinations from Orlando.

Deep South Airways appreciates your continued patronage and is offering a new member discount using our site to book flights to and through Orlando in April and May. You may book connecting flights on other airlines right on our webpage. When using our website, enter the discount ----3---- "MCO20" for 20% off all fares.

We handle All-Florida and other Southern carrier flights at the most ----4---- rates. Thank you again for choosing us.

1. (A) Flights to Florida are more accessible than ever.
　　(B) Deep South Airlines has serviced Atlanta for 20 years.
　　(C) Please be advised that some routes have changed.
　　(D) Atlanta to Memphis is eligible for the greatest discount.

Ⓐ Ⓑ Ⓒ Ⓓ

2. (A) reset　　　　　　　(B) relocate
　　(C) transport　　　　　(D) transfer

Ⓐ Ⓑ Ⓒ Ⓓ

3. (A) code　　　　　　　(B) pass
　　(C) share　　　　　　(D) tour

Ⓐ Ⓑ Ⓒ Ⓓ

4. (A) compete　　　　　　(B) competition
　　(C) competitive　　　　(D) competitor

Ⓐ Ⓑ Ⓒ Ⓓ

Part 7　読解問題

設問の解答として最も適切なものを選んでください。

Advertisement

It's Gym Time
NEWLY OPENED

Welcome to a new concept in gym membership. At IGT, you set the pace. Our trainers are not body builders; instead, they are ordinary folks who have made good health and exercise a part of their lives. We know you're busy, so there's no need to keep to a schedule. IGT is open 24 hours a day, seven days a week. We also have a juice bar and an Olympic-size swimming pool and spa to make every visit a relaxing one. Couples/Family Memberships available. Call 555-0193 or check us out online at IGT.com today.

Review

IGT.com　47 Reviews ★★★★

Screen name: littleswan497 ★★★★☆
I recently joined IGT and I'm mostly satisfied with the experience.

They have up-to-date equipment and trainers who understand ordinary working people. However, I wish they would use less harsh chemicals in the pool--the chlorine is strong. I'd also love a separate exercise area for women. I used to belong to a "women only" gym and liked that privacy. Their juice bar is great, but it would be nice if they sold healthy meals, as well. I wish they would consider price breaks for groups of friends. Their only discount plan seems to be for relatives.

Fairfield Business Buzz

by Jordan Richter

Three months ago, IGT opened in Fairfield. It was the first new gym in a long time. In fact, the most recent trend has seen gyms closing and home exercise equipment on the rise. The obvious success of this business can be attributed to a few ways that IGT sets themselves apart from other gyms. First of all, they are not pushing a glamorous body agenda. Next, they are always open, so there is no need for potential clients to worry about how to fit the gym into their schedule. Finally, and perhaps most important of all, they are very responsive to user feedback.

Based on client input, they have set up a space where women can exercise privately, they have arranged for groups of friends to register and take advantage of group discounts, they have added some larger lockers for personal item storage, and they have converted the pool to one with a bromine cleaning system, which is said to be much easier on skin and hair than chlorine. They appear to be one of the fastest growing businesses in the area.

1. What does the advertisement suggest about the gym?

(A) It is managed by a family.

(B) It closes early on weekends.

(C) It offers its users flexibility.

(D) It is frequented by body builders.

Ⓐ Ⓑ Ⓒ Ⓓ

2. In paragraph 1, line 4 of the advertisement, the word "keep" is closest in meaning to

(A) enjoy   (B) guard

(C) own   (D) stick

Ⓐ Ⓑ Ⓒ Ⓓ

3. What does *littleswan497* imply about the trainers?

(A) They can be harsh.

(B) They understand people like her.

(C) They have very full schedules.

(D) They give her special exercises.

Ⓐ Ⓑ Ⓒ Ⓓ

4. Which of the recent improvements at IGT was NOT suggested by
   littleswan497?
   (A) The new cleaning system
   (B) The bigger lockers
   (C) The group memberships
   (D) The private women's section

   (A) (B) (C) (D)

5. What seems to impress Mr. Richter about the gym?
   (A) The pool is quite large.
   (B) They have highly trained instructors.
   (C) They listen to user comments.
   (D) The interior is quite glamorous.

   (A) (B) (C) (D)

On the Agenda
—Meetings & Schedules
議題―会議・スケジュール

Parts 1–4 Listening

Sound Advice

How の疑問文の聞き取り

　How には、様々な質問の可能性が含まれていて、それがさらに別の単語と組み合わさって疑問文を作ります。そのため、答え方も複雑で予測がしにくいのです。

―文頭に最大限の注意を払おう―
How ではじまる疑問文でよく用いられるものは以下の通りです。

　How ...?　どのようにして、どんな状態で
　　How's the weather where you're from?

　How much/ How many...?　どれくらい（の量、金額・数）
　　How many items do you want to order?

　How far ...?　どのくらいの距離で
　　How far is the nearest station from here?

　How come ...?　なぜ =why
　　How come you never talk to him?

　How often ...?　どのくらいの頻度で
　　How often do you call on that client?

　How else ...?　他にどうしたら、他に何が（選択肢）
　　How else can we create effective proposals?

　How about ...?　はどうですか（提案）
　　How about having a meeting?

● **Exercise**

CD 3-02〜07

1〜6の解答として最も適切なものをA〜Fの中から選んでください。

1. ( )
2. ( )
3. ( )
4. ( )
5. ( )
6. ( )

A. Once every three months
B. I can't stand it.
C. There are only four of us.
D. Charge more for the product
E. Ten minutes by bus
F. Just another minute or two

Vocabulary Warm–up

オフィスで働く人の状況を示す表現

それぞれの状況を示す表現の訳として正しいものをA〜Jの中から選び、その記号を（　　）の中に記入してください。

1. at one's desk　　　　　( )
2. in a meeting　　　　　( )
3. off for the day　　　　( )
4. on a conference call　( )
5. on the phone　　　　( )
6. on one's way to 〜　　( )
7. at a conference　　　( )
8. out of the office　　　( )
9. out sick　　　　　　　( )
10. on leave　　　　　　( )

A. (公式な)会議の場で
B. 席についている（執務中で）
C. 席を外している（外出中で）
D. 会議中で
E. 休暇中で
F. 本日の業務終了で
G. 電話会議中で
H. 電話中で
I. 〜に向かっている途中で
J. 病欠で

Part 1　写真描写問題

写真について最も適切なものを選んでください。

🎧 3-08、09

1.

Ⓐ Ⓑ Ⓒ Ⓓ

2.

Ⓐ Ⓑ Ⓒ Ⓓ

Part 2　応答問題

質問の応答として最も適切なものを選んでください。

🎧 3-10〜13

1. Mark your answer.　　Ⓐ Ⓑ Ⓒ

2. Mark your answer.　　Ⓐ Ⓑ Ⓒ

3. Mark your answer.　　Ⓐ Ⓑ Ⓒ

4. Mark your answer.　　Ⓐ Ⓑ Ⓒ

Part 3 会話問題 ....

設問の解答として最も適切なものを選んでください。

3-14、15

1. What is the man's main point?

(A) He is relieved to hear that Trevor went to the conference.

(B) He is very worried about Myra's illness.

(C) He thinks that this meeting is a waste of time.

(D) He is happy to have this chance to meet with Jane.

Ⓐ Ⓑ Ⓒ Ⓓ

2. What does the woman want to talk about?

(A) Sending employees to conferences

(B) Employees taking sick leave

(C) Amount of current sales

(D) Purchases of desktop computers

Ⓐ Ⓑ Ⓒ Ⓓ

3. What will they most likely do next?

(A) Keep on with their meeting in this room

(B) Move to the woman's office for a discussion

(C) Phone Trevor so he can join by teleconference

(D) Discuss which conferences employees should attend

Ⓐ Ⓑ Ⓒ Ⓓ

Part 4 説明文問題 ....

設問の解答として最も適切なものを選んでください。

3-16、17

1. What is the main purpose of the meeting?

(A) To discuss some details about the film

(B) To take them to a Japanese restaurant

(C) To discuss their ideas for advertising

(D) To introduce some of their new staff members

Ⓐ Ⓑ Ⓒ Ⓓ

2. What does the woman imply when she says, "He said he could clear his calendar on either day"?

(A) Mr. Nelson is not quite sure about his schedule yet.

(B) Mr. Nelson's schedule is clear the first day.

(C) Mr. Nelson is not free the second day.

(D) Mr. Nelson is free to meet on either day.

Ⓐ　Ⓑ　Ⓒ　Ⓓ

3. When will they go to the Japanese restaurant?

(A) This evening

(B) Tomorrow evening

(C) On Wednesday afternoon

(D) On Friday afternoon

Ⓐ　Ⓑ　Ⓒ　Ⓓ

Parts 5–7 Reading

Grammar Review

頻度を表す副詞

頻度のパーセンテージ

100% always
　　　 almost always, frequently
　　　 usually, often, regularly
50% sometimes
　　　 occasionally
　　　 rarely, hardly ever, seldom
0% never

語順

基本的に以下のように使われます。

1) 一般動詞の前 (否定形のときは not の前)

　例) I often attend the conference.
　　　 I usually do not drink coffee at night.

2) be 動詞のときは動詞の後（否定形のときは not の後）

　例) Japanese trains are always on time.
　　　 Weather forecasts are not always right.

3）現在完了形は have の後

例）I have never gone on a trip overseas.

注）頻度の低い hardly ever, seldom, really といった副詞は、否定的な意味をもつので動詞は否定形を伴いません。

誤）I seldom don't eat out.

正）I seldom eat out.

● **Exercise**

では実際に頻度をあらわす副詞についての問題を解いてください。
次のランダムにならんだ単語を並べ替えて、正しい文章にしてください。

1. never have read report this

   We ＿＿＿＿ ＿＿＿＿ ＿＿＿＿ anything like ＿＿＿＿ ＿＿＿＿ .

2. is open   meeting room sometimes special

   This ＿＿＿＿ ＿＿＿＿ ＿＿＿＿ ＿＿＿＿ ＿＿＿＿ ＿＿＿＿ to the public.

3. usually speak the   don't to audience

   I ＿＿＿＿ ＿＿＿＿ ＿＿＿＿ ＿＿＿＿ ＿＿＿＿ ＿＿＿＿ before my presentation.

4. in morning not the is always

   He ＿＿＿＿ ＿＿＿＿ ＿＿＿＿ in the office ＿＿＿＿ ＿＿＿＿ ＿＿＿＿ .

Mini Practice Test

Part 5 文法問題

文を完成するのに最も適切なものを選んでください。

1. Because my boss is so stubborn, I ------ have a reasonable conversation with him.

   (A) always   (B) sometimes

   (C) all the time   (D) rarely

   Ⓐ Ⓑ Ⓒ Ⓓ

2. Our class is every night, Monday through Friday, so you can say we meet ------ .

(A) often

(B) rarely

(C) once in a while

(D) occasionally

Ⓐ Ⓑ Ⓒ Ⓓ

3. I get so bored with my routine because I ------ eat the same thing for lunch.

(A) never

(B) almost always

(C) once a week

(D) seldom

Ⓐ Ⓑ Ⓒ Ⓓ

Part 6　長文穴埋め問題

文を完成するのに最も適切なものを選んでください。

The Seattle chapter of the Young Entrepreneurs Society (YES) is holding its annual mini-conference in the weekend of September 14, 15. This has been hailed as one of the most ---**1.**--- youth events of the year. There will be a keynote speaker, two featured speakers, workshops and informal ---**2.**--- groups throughout the weekend. It is still possible to attend the conference. ---**3.**--- . Just go to "Seattle.YES.com" and click on "Regional Conference." This year, we have invited Dr. Merrill D. Cho of The Seoul School of Management to ---**4.**--- the opening speech. Her topic is "Creating New Businesses in a Crowded Market."

1. (A) excite　　　　　　(B) excited

(C) excitement　　　(D) exciting

Ⓐ Ⓑ Ⓒ Ⓓ

2. (A) discuss　　　　　(B) discussed

(C) discussion　　　(D) discussions

Ⓐ Ⓑ Ⓒ Ⓓ

3. (A) Therefore, contact Dr. Cho for information.

   (B) However, the deadline to register is July 10.

   (C) For this reason, the previous conference was successful.

   (D) Nonetheless, there are over 150 members in the chapter.

   Ⓐ Ⓑ Ⓒ Ⓓ

4. (A) deduct   (B) deliver

   (C) receive   (D) signal

   Ⓐ Ⓑ Ⓒ Ⓓ

| **Part 7**   読解問題 | ··· |

設問の解答として最も適切なものを選んでください。

Text-message Chain

Melanie Cardini   [10:01 A.M.]

Good morning everyone. I'd like to get your input on what to emphasize when promoting our spring line-up.

Danielle Gorman   [10:02 A.M.]

Right, you folks are meeting with the ad agency this afternoon…

Melanie Cardini   [10:03 A.M.]

Yeah, at 2:00, if anyone else will be downtown today, you're welcome to join us.

Will Griffin   [10:03 A.M.]

I can't make that meeting, but I have a few notes. Except for our new kids' jeans, most of our standard items are the same as last year. So, I say we focus on what's new.

Jodie Nakagawa   [10:02 A.M.]

Of course, that makes sense, but our straight leg, so-called "skinny jeans" have sold more than any other item in the past year… They're popular among both men and women, so we may even want to do some rebranding, calling them unisex jeans. I don't want to leave them out of the ads entirely

---

> **Melanie Cardini**   [10:04 A.M.]
> I'll make sure we focus on our entire line of jeans.

> **Will Griffin**   [10:06 A.M.]
> What is definitely different this year is the array of colors, especially in the children's line. We've got some citrus colors—greens, yellows, oranges… And we seem to be selling a lot of black jeans to adults this year, so we need them to highlight these points.

> **Melanie Cardini**   [10:07 A.M.]
> I have some great adult shots from the last fashion show we attended in Paris. I'll bring along my photo album to give the creative company some ideas. We should get them to come up with ideas for shooting local kids wearing our line.

1. For what kind of company do these people most likely work?
   (A) An advertising company
   (B) An electronics company
   (C) A fashion company
   (D) A toy company

   Ⓐ Ⓑ Ⓒ Ⓓ

2. What does Mr. Griffin mean when he says, "I have a few notes"?
   (A) He wants to write down everything they say.
   (B) He wants to offer them his opinion.
   (C) He would like to change the meeting time.
   (D) He thinks they should find another agency.

   Ⓐ Ⓑ Ⓒ Ⓓ

3. What does Melanie plan to do at the meeting?
   (A) Wear a sample of the company's jeans
   (B) Show them some pictures from France
   (C) Teleconference with Will on her computer
   (D) Ask the company to focus on adult styles only

   Ⓐ Ⓑ Ⓒ Ⓓ

At the Office —Negotiating & Selling

オフィス─交渉・販売

Parts 1–4 Listening

Sound Advice

単語を見極める ─同音異義語（homonyms）─

● **Just listen** 3-19〜21

まず意味を確かめながら、1 〜 12 の発音をしっかり聞いてください。音声は標準的なアメリカ英語の発音によるものです。

同音異義語

1	ad	広告	add	加える
2	close	閉じる	clothes	衣服
3	for	〜のために	four	4（数字）
4	cruise	船旅をする（数か所を巡る）	crews	乗組員（複数）
5	hear	聞く	here	ここ（場所）
6	nose	鼻	knows	知る（三人称単数形）
7	one	1（数字）	won	勝った（過去形）
8	plain	簡素な	plane	飛行機
9	some	いくつかの	sum	合計
10	wait	待つ	weight	重さ
11	who's	who has, who is の短縮形	whose	誰の
12	your	あなたの	you're	you are の短縮形

● Exercise

通常、ほとんどの同音異義語は文の状況から判断して、どちらの単語が使われているかを区別することができます。

1〜8の短い英文を聞いてください。AかBのどちらの意味で使われているかを文脈から判断して、使われている方の単語を選んでください。

	A	B		
1.	cruise	crews	(	)
2.	cruise	crews	(	)
3.	close	clothes	(	)
4.	one	won	(	)
5.	some	sum	(	)
6.	wait	weight	(	)
7.	close	clothes	(	)
8.	plain	plane	(	)

Vocabulary Warm-up

意思決定 (decision making) や合意 (agreement) に役立つ表現

以下は、会議などでよく用いられる表現のリストです。

agree with/go with	〜に同意する
against/for	（人の意見や物事に）〜に反対して、賛成して
across the board	全体［全般・全て］にわたって、全体的に、全面的に
consensus	（集団の）意見の一致、合意
decision	決定
in favor of/in support of	〜に賛成して、〜を支持して
pick	選択する
a show of hands	挙手（による意思表示）
unanimous	満場一致の
vote for	〜に賛成の投票をする
weigh in	加勢する、介入する
where one stands	自分の立場

● **Exercise**

1〜6の空所にあてはまる語句を (A) 〜 (F) の中から選んでください。

1. The reason we're asking is we want to know _____ .

2. It is very difficult for the world's nations to come to _____ on this issue.

3. I knew the group was in total agreement because the vote was _____ .

4. I don't want to make a final decision until we ask Mr. Price to _____ .

5. We decided to _____ the cheaper hotel, because the group wanted to have value over comfort.

6. Accepting what you say, I'm still _____ the project proposal.

(A) weigh in	(B) go with	(C) a consensus
(D) where you stand	(E) unanimous	(F) against

Mini Practice Test

Part 1　写真描写問題 ....

写真について最も適切なものを選んでください。

 3-30、31

1.

Ⓐ Ⓑ Ⓒ Ⓓ

2.

Ⓐ Ⓑ Ⓒ Ⓓ

Part 2　応答問題

質問の応答として最も適切なものを選んでください。

 3-32～35

1. Mark your answer. 　　 (A) (B) (C)

2. Mark your answer. 　　 (A) (B) (C)

3. Mark your answer. 　　 (A) (B) (C)

4. Mark your answer. 　　 (A) (B) (C)

Part 3　会話問題

設問の解答として最も適切なものを選んでください。

 3-36、37

1. Who most likely is the woman?
   (A) The company president
   (B) Someone in upper management
   (C) A middle manager
   (D) A regular employee

(A) (B) (C) (D)

2. What does the man mean when he says, "I agree that we tend to be very generous"?
   (A) He believes their company treats employees with kindness.
   (B) He thinks that the board members are all gentlemen.
   (C) He believes that the company offers employees good money.
   (D) He thinks that the company should give more to charity.

(A) (B) (C) (D)

3. What will most likely happen after this discussion?
   (A) They will agree to give all employees more money.
   (B) They will eliminate raises to save money.
   (C) They will just give extra money to those in middle management and lower.
   (D) They will arrange for pay increases for upper management only.

(A) (B) (C) (D)

$\boxed{\textbf{Part 4} \quad \text{説明文問題}}$ ....

設問の解答として最も適切なものを選んでください。 3-38、39

1. According to this talk, who can benefit from their tour packages?

    (A) Just about any traveler

    (B) Just travelers on a tight budget

    (C) Mostly travelers with little experience

    (D) Only travelers with unusual interests

    Ⓐ Ⓑ © Ⓓ

2. What idea does this talk most strongly promote?

    (A) Inexpensive airfare and hotel accommodations

    (B) Eco tours and environmentally friendly trips

    (C) Choices in accordance with the traveler's wishes

    (D) All types of transportation and hotels

    Ⓐ Ⓑ © Ⓓ

3. What does the speaker imply when she says, "Why not go old-school"?

    (A) Listeners should consider going back to using a travel agent.

    (B) The company is offering a special price for older travelers.

    (C) It is possible to get a student discount with this travel agency.

    (D) The agency has a special school for people interested in eco tours.

    Ⓐ Ⓑ © Ⓓ

Grammar Review

現在完了の用法

現在完了 [have/has + 動詞の過去分詞] は以下の場合に使われます。

1. 過去の経験　いつのことかはっきりしない過去の動作や状況を述べます。

　★よく一緒に使われる already, ever, never は過去分詞の前に入ります。

　例） I **have** (I've) *already* **read** this report.

　　　I **have** (I've) *never* **talked** to him.

　★　よく一緒に使われる yet は文の最後に入ります。

　例） I **have** (I've) **not watched** it *yet*.

2. 継続　過去に始まり、今も続いている動作や状況を述べます。

　★一緒に使われるのは today や this week など（まだ終わっていない時間・期限）で、yesterday, five minutes ago, last week など（すでに終わった時間・期限）は使いません。

　例） He **has** (He's) **visited** the client office twice **this week**.

　★ for と since はよく現在完了に使われます。

　例） I **have** (I've) **worked in** this office **for** thirty years.

　　　I **have** (I've) **worked** here **since** 1990.

3. ごく最近の出来事

　★ 一緒に使われるのは just です。

　例） She **has** (She's) *just* **arrived** here.

● Exercise

では実際に現在完了についての問題を解いてください。

１～５の文章の下線部に、（　　　　）内のランダムに並んだ単語を入れて文章を完成してください。

　1. (never, have, been)

　　We ＿＿＿＿＿＿ ＿＿＿＿＿＿ ＿＿＿＿＿＿ to Chef Luke's original restaurant in New York, but we like the one here.

　2 (yet, approved, not, has, been)

　　That budget ＿＿＿＿＿＿ ＿＿＿＿＿＿ ＿＿＿＿＿＿ ＿＿＿＿＿＿ ＿＿＿＿＿＿.

3. (just, arrived, has)

The guest of honor _____ _____ _____ in front of the conference room.

4. (today, has, watched, twice)

He _____ _____ the same promotion video _____ _____.

5. (he, lived, was, has, since)

Jack _____ _____ in Tokyo_____ _____ _____ a teenager.

Mini Practice Test

Part 5 文法問題 ....

文を完成するのに最も適切なものを選んでください。

1. It's so hot that, unfortunately, some of the candy letters on the birthday cake ------ melted in the sun.
   (A) has   (B) have
   (C) is   (D) be

   Ⓐ Ⓑ Ⓒ Ⓓ

2. I've ------ checked the sales plan several times for mistakes, but I'd like to proofread it one more time before the meeting.
   (A) already   (B) ever
   (C) never   (D) yet

   Ⓐ Ⓑ Ⓒ Ⓓ

3. While Sue and Glenn have traveled to Italy many times, they ------ spent time in Rome in summer.
   (A) have never   (B) have ever
   (C) did   (D) were

   Ⓐ Ⓑ Ⓒ Ⓓ

文を完成するのに最も適切なものを選んでください。

Dear Patron,

Thank you for your contribution to the Sunset Maritime Museum. Our efforts to pass on our rich seacoast history to the next generation have been a phenomenal success. We were able to raise more than $60,000 this past year. ----**1.**----
There are many projects in progress and more planned for the following year. ----**2.**---- , several retired sea captains have been volunteering their time for live storytelling sessions, which have been getting young people interested in boating and fishing.

Consequently, we hope to exceed the amount of donations this coming year. An anonymous donor has contributed $20,000 to get the ball ----**3.**---- . We are delighted about this, as we anticipate remodeling costs of $100,000.

We understand that everyone's resources are limited, ----**4.**---- we ask that you help us spread the word by forwarding this to your family, friends and associates. The Sunset Maritime Museum is a worthy cause. Since the museum reopened, the number of people staying and working in this town after high school, as well as those attending college and coming back here to work in family businesses has increased almost 10%. Help save our local heritage. Your help will be appreciated for generations to come.

1. (A) Actually, there were at least a dozen new projects involving seabirds.
   (B) On the other hand, we didn't finish the report to our shareholders in time.
   (C) Otherwise, there was no information about the matter that could be shared.
   (D) Nonetheless, we project we will need further funding to meet operating costs.

Ⓐ Ⓑ Ⓒ Ⓓ

2. (A) For example,
   (B) However,
   (C) Notwithstanding,
   (D) On the other hand,

Ⓐ Ⓑ Ⓒ Ⓓ

3. (A) roll   (B) rolled

    (C) rolling   (D) rolls

Ⓐ Ⓑ Ⓒ Ⓓ

4. (A) for   (B) unless

    (C) but   (D) so

Ⓐ Ⓑ Ⓒ Ⓓ

Part 7   読解問題 ···

設問の解答として最も適切なものを選んでください。

Estimate

Approximate Distance of move: 117 miles		
	Lower Estimate	**Upper Estimate**
Estimated Weight:	12,420 lbs.	15,525 lbs.
Transportation Expenses:	$3,521	$3,700
Packing Expenses:	$1,873	$2,341
Total Cost:	**$5,394**	**$6,041**

Letter

Roy Olsen, Director
Olsen Moving Co.
5201 Mallard Road, Suite 1
San Diego, CA 92120
619-555-0920

Jason and Terry Harper
9033 Oriole St.
Lemon Grove, CA 91945

Dear Jason and Terry,

We have calculated costs based on the number of furnished rooms you have and the number of people living in your home. During our conversation over the phone, we discussed your packing some boxes yourselves. For every ten pounds of packed boxes that you pre-pack, we can offer you a $2 discount off of the total weight charge. To reduce total weight charges even further, you may consider renting a self-packing trailer for moving the items you wish to pack yourselves.

We do suggest that you let us pack dishes, works of art, furniture, etc., so that it will arrive at your new home in the same condition that it leaves. In our long experience, we have learned that our professional packers can prevent damage to your valuables. If we need to move any oversized objects, such as pianos, large screen TVs, boats, etc., there will be an additional surcharge.

At Olsen, we promise the best service at the most competitive rates. If you get a lower quote, from another company, please show it to us and we will try to beat it. We pride ourselves on good, honest service.

Kindest regards,

Roy Olsen

Roy Olsen

1. What is the purpose of the letter?
   (A) To finalize the agreement to move the family's things.
   (B) To give the family an estimate on moving their things.
   (C) To explain to the family why something got broken during the move.
   (D) To recommend another company to handle the family's move.

2. If their goods weigh the higher amount and they pack 150 pounds themselves, what will their final total be?
   (A) $5394
   (B) $5741
   (C) $6011
   (D) $6041

3. What does Mr. Olsen imply about items that could break easily?

(A) Breakage will not be the mover's fault.

(B) The owner should take care of them.

(C) They should be in their original boxes.

(D) The movers should pack them.

Ⓐ Ⓑ Ⓒ Ⓓ

4. The word "beat," in paragraph 3, line 3, is closest in meaning to

(A) outdo

(B) unhand

(C) overstep

(D) upset

Ⓐ Ⓑ Ⓒ Ⓓ

5. Why does Mr. Olsen mention renting self-packing trailers and talking to other companies?

(A) He owns several companies and is trying to get business one way or the other.

(B) He thinks the client has not done enough research when it comes to moving costs.

(C) He believes that good and honest service means saving people money.

(D) The Harpers probably have more things than will fit in Mr. Olsen's moving vans.

Ⓐ Ⓑ Ⓒ Ⓓ

During the Interview
—Job Hunting & Self-promotion

面接—就活・自己PR

Parts 1–4 Listening

Sound Advice

状況をイメージする

リスニングセクションで大切なのは聞いた内容から状況をイメージするスキルを磨くことです。

● Exercise

CD 3-41~45

以下の (A) ~ (E) に目を通してください。次に1~5のスクリプトを聞き、状況にあてはまる番号を (　) の中に記入してください。

(A) Someone explaining how to use a new device. 　　　(　　)

(B) People setting up some sort of reception. 　　　(　　)

(C) A person helping with someone else's job preparation. (　　)

(D) People having some sort of business discussion. 　　　(　　)

(E) Someone taking a candidate to a waiting room. 　　　(　　)

Vocabulary Tips

ビジネスでよく用いられる略語 (Business Acronyms)

次の1~6までの表現は、インタビューによく用いられます。

1. **BOD**: board of directors　　　　取締役会、役員会
2. **BOT**: board of trustees　　　　評議員会 (BOD と類似するもの)
3. **CEO**: chief executive officer　　最高経営責任者 (会社のトップに位置する人)
4. **CFO**: chief financial officer　　最高財務責任者
5. **HR**: human resources　　　　　人事部
6. **R&D**: research and development　研究開発部

Vocabulary Warm-up

感謝の意を示す表現

感謝の気持ちを示す表現には色々なものがありますが、ここでは特にビジネスの場面でよく用いられるものをまとめました。

· I'm **thankful/grateful for** the chance to be part of the team.

· I'm **thankful/grateful** to you for your advice.

· **Thank you for** making this conference such a success.

· I **wish to thank** everyone for coming today.

· The employers got together to **give thanks** for all the help they received from the town's people.

· I'd like to **express my gratitude** for the opportunity to speak here today.

· I **appreciate** everything you've done for me.

· We have given all the employees a special bonus **to show our appreciation**.

● Exercise

2〜6までの空所にあてはまる語句を（A）〜（F）の中から選んでください。
(A) show one's appreciation と (B) express one's gratitude の場合は、代名詞を文脈に合うように変えてください。なお、正解は1つとは限りません。
注）No. 1 はすでに解答されています。

1. It's the least I can do to (A) show my appreciation.

2. We are _____ to the group of workers who stayed all night and set up the display room.

3. The purpose of the speech was for the president to _____ to all the employees who volunteered at the event.

4. We'd like to _____ for all their hard work.

5. The man was so _____ when I returned his lost wallet.

6. I really _____ your quick reply.

(A) show (one's) appreciation	(B) express (one's) gratitude
(C) give thanks	(D) grateful
(E) appreciate	(F) thankful

Mini Practice Test

Part 1　写真描写問題 ....

写真について最も適切なものを選んでください。

🎧 3-46、47

1.

Ⓐ Ⓑ Ⓒ Ⓓ

2.

Ⓐ Ⓑ Ⓒ Ⓓ

Part 2　応答問題 ....

設問の応答として最も適切なものを選んでください。

🎧 3-48～51

1. Mark your answer.　　Ⓐ Ⓑ Ⓒ

2. Mark your answer.　　Ⓐ Ⓑ Ⓒ

3. Mark your answer.　　Ⓐ Ⓑ Ⓒ

4. Mark your answer.　　Ⓐ Ⓑ Ⓒ

Part 3　会話問題 ....

設問の応答として最も適切なものを選んでください。 3-52、53

1. Where does this conversation most likely take place?
   (A) At the main office
   (B) At a branch office
   (C) In the woman's office
   (D) At a manufacturing facility

2. In which part of the company does the woman currently work?
   (A) In the Product Support Department
   (B) At the manufacturing facility
   (C) For the Human Resources Department
   (D) In the Research and Development Department

3. What does the woman imply about future work at the main headquarters?
   (A) Doing that would not be her first choice.
   (B) That is one of the places she would be willing to work.
   (C) She thinks such work is more important than working elsewhere.
   (D) She is afraid there is too much competition for jobs there.

   Ⓐ Ⓑ Ⓒ Ⓓ

設問の応答として最も適切なものを選んでください。

 3-54、55

Job Offerings

Job Category	Employer	Education	Start
Tour Guide	City Tourism Bureau	Bachelor's/ associate's degree in Tourism	October
Financial Specialist	Dept. of Finance	Master's degree in finance	September
Advertising Copywriter	Mumford Advertising	Bachelor's degree in English/journalism	September
Professorship	Sherman City University	Ph.D. in sociology	September

1. Who would be interested in this information?

(A) Companies that need to hire new employees.

(B) People who are looking for a job.

(C) People who are self-employed.

(D) New employees at the City Job Center.

Ⓐ Ⓑ Ⓒ Ⓓ

2. How would someone make use of the City Job Center's services?

(A) By visiting their office at any time.

(B) By going to work in their office

(C) By inviting a representative to visit their home

(D) By scheduling a meeting at their office

Ⓐ Ⓑ Ⓒ Ⓓ

3. Look at the graphic. Which position shows information that differs from what was announced?

(A) The tour guide

(B) The financial specialist

(C) The advertising copywriter

(D) The professorship

Parts 5–7 Reading

Grammar Review

仮定法の用法

● **仮定法過去**

現在起きてないこと、現実には叶えられない望みなどを表すときに用いられます。

条件節		主　節		
If	(be 動詞) 主語＋ **were**	主語	would, should should, could might	(be 動詞) **原形**
If	(do 動詞) 主語＋**過去形**			(do 動詞) **原形**

be 動詞

例) If he **were** to tell the police every detail about the incident, his name **would be** cleared.

do 動詞

例) If I **knew** the details about his incident, I **could tell** them to the police instead of him.

● **仮定法過去完了**

現在の時点において、過去に起こったこととは違うことを表します。

条件節		主　節		
If	(be 動詞) 主語＋ **had been**	主語	would, should should, could might	(be 動詞) (do 動詞) **have + 過去分詞**
If	(do 動詞) 主語＋**過去完了**			

be 動詞

例）If I **had been** more experienced, I **would have explained** the intent of the question.

do 動詞

例）If he **had behaved** modestly, his presentation **would have been accepted** by everyone.

● 仮定法現在

提案、主張、要求、命令などを表す動詞の後にくる that 節の中で用いられます。

例）The lawyer **recommends** <u>that</u> he **tell** the police every detail about the incident.

● **Exercise**

では実際に仮定法についての問題を解いてください。

次の下線部の（A）〜（F）に be 動詞の正しい活用形を記入して文を完成してください。

1. Margaret wishes that she ____(A)____ able to explain the project to the boss better.

2. I suggested to Jim that Ms. Berman ____(B)____ invited to the conference in Los Angeles.

3. If I ____(C)____ younger, I would go back to school and study to become a doctor.

4. I sometimes think it might ____(D)____ better for everyone in this project team if I ____(E)____ not here.

5. I'm not sure what she would do if Gloria ____(F)____ to get the job that she has already applied for five times.

Mini Practice Test

Part 5　文法問題

文を完成するのに最も適切なものを選んでください。

1. I often wish I ------ efficient enough to make a higher salary and take a trip around the world.
   (A) be   (B) am
   (C) are   (D) were

   Ⓐ Ⓑ Ⓒ Ⓓ

2. If he acted more confidently, his ideas ------ taken more seriously by scientists who took part in the conference.
   (A) will be   (B) would be
   (A) have been   (D) can be

   Ⓐ Ⓑ Ⓒ Ⓓ

3. If I ------ closer attention, I would have seen that I forgot to add one of the letters of recommendation to the resume that I sent to the company.
   (A) was paid
   (B) have paid
   (C) have been paying
   (D) had been paying

   Ⓐ Ⓑ Ⓒ Ⓓ

文を完成するのに最も適切なものを選んでください。

Paid Student Internship

Hutchins Event Planning and Promotion is searching for someone interested in the ------- of promotion and event planning. Three to six-week internships are
1.
available during regular college spring, summer and winter breaks. No experience is ------- , but prior study in the areas of marketing, advertising,
2.
journalism or creative writing is preferred. After completing the short online job application at www.huchevent.com/internship, we ask that each applicant -------
3.
a short essay to the site, following the stated instructions. Rather than scheduling a face-to-face interview, our creative department will be video conferencing with all applicants that make our short list. Our creative director, Sophia Dietrich, is happy to answer any questions you may have. Please e-mail her at sdietrich@huchevent.com. Our goal is reach out to those interested in a future in event planning. -------
4.

We thank you in advance for your cooperation.

Kind regards,
Bryce Kendall
Management

1. (A) entities   (B) fields
   (B) places   (D) territories

Ⓐ Ⓑ Ⓒ Ⓓ

2. (A) necessary   (B) necessitated
   (C) necessitating   (D) necessity

Ⓐ Ⓑ Ⓒ Ⓓ

3. (A) upload   (B) uploaded
   (C) uploading   (D) uploads

Ⓐ Ⓑ Ⓒ Ⓓ

4. (A) I apologize for the short turn-around time of this notice.

(B) So, let us know when to schedule your face-to-face interview.

(C) So, make sure you possess a strong background in marketing.

(D) So, feel free to pass this information on to possible candidates.

Ⓐ Ⓑ Ⓒ Ⓓ

Part 7 　読解問題

設問の応答として最も適切なものを選んでください。

E-mail

Richard Marcus
United Industrial Design Associates
6734 Wilson Ave.
Boulder, CO 80301
richardm@inter.com

Dear Mr. Marcus,

We met briefly at the job placement fair and I took your business card. I am interested in arranging to interview at your company. I graduated from Colorado Institute of Technology with a degree in industrial engineering. Right after graduation I took a year off to travel and work briefly in Europe, spending much of the time in Spain and France. For the past few years I have been teaching basic engineering at North Ridge Technical High School and taking courses toward my master's degree at night. Working with teenagers has been an amazing education for me, but I feel my talents would be better suited to the corporate world. I get along very well with my colleagues and they are surprised that I am choosing to leave. From what you explained to me the day we met, your company is the most active organization in the field of industrial design in this region. I find industrial design fascinating and I would like to work in this field. I went to the job fair thinking that I might end up staying in my teaching position but talking with you inspired me to make a change.

Please let me know if it would be possible to come in for an interview sometime soon. Thank you in advance.

Best regards,

Blane Markowitz
7640 Niles Dr.
Yuma, CO 80759

Resume

Blane L. Markowitz

7640 Niles Dr.
Yuma, CO 80759
blmarkowitz@greywolf.zz.com
https://linkedin.com/in/brett-l-markowitz

OBJECTIVE: Work in an industrial design firm

Current high school engineering instructor seeking opportunities to research, create and market in corporate industrial design.

EDUCATION AND TECHNICAL SKILLS

Northeastern Colorado State University
Masters in EDI (Engineering Design Innovation) Expected May 2021
Colorado Institute of Technology
Bachelor of Science in Engineering (June 2017), GPA 3.8
- Studied manufacturing and design engineering
- Had a minor proficiency in robotics
- Studied Spanish for six semesters; French for four semesters

PROFESSIONAL EXPERIENCE

September 2018-Present
  North Ridge Technical High School
    - Taught Engineering and physics
May-August 2016
  Miller Design (Internship)
    - Tested new products
    - Suggested mechanical and style improvements

LEADERSHIP

President of the University Cross-Cultural Club—organized meetings and events in a club with 30% international students. (To continue my interest in the international scene, I spent a year traveling in Europe. Throughout the year I did part-time jobs at restaurants, stores and factories.)

References and transcripts available upon request.

1. What is the main point of this e-mail?
(A) Mr. Markowitz wants to get a job at Mr. Marcus's company.
(B) Mr. Markowitz wants to submit an industrial design to Mr. Marcus.
(C) The recipient wrote to Mr. Markowitz first and this is his reply.
(D) The writer wants Mr. Marcus to speak at his high school.

Ⓐ Ⓑ Ⓒ Ⓓ

2. What is Mr. Markowitz currently doing?
(A) He is a university student.
(B) He is at a different design company.
(C) He is working at the job placement fair.
(D) He is teaching at a high school.

Ⓐ Ⓑ Ⓒ Ⓓ

3. What is suggested about Mr. Markowitz' reaction to his conversation with Mr. Marcus?
(A) He was inspired to pursue a new career.
(B) He was surprised at how much he liked teaching.
(C) He was amazed at how famous Mr. Marcus was.
(D) He was concerned about the financial state of Mr. Marcus's company.

Ⓐ Ⓑ Ⓒ Ⓓ

4. What does the resume suggest about why he spent so much of his stay in Spain and France?
(A) He was particularly interested in industrial design in those countries.
(B) He accompanied some high school students to those countries.
(C) Some friends from his club invited him to come to those countries.
(D) He has studied the languages spoken in those countries.

Ⓐ Ⓑ Ⓒ Ⓓ

5. In the LEADERSHIP section of the resume, line 3, the word "spent" is closest in meaning to
(A) drained energy   (B) invested time
(C) used money   (D) wasted effort

Ⓐ Ⓑ Ⓒ Ⓓ

※コピーしてお使いください。

LISTENING SECTION

Unit 1

Part 1

No.	Answer
1	Ⓐ Ⓑ Ⓒ Ⓓ
2	Ⓐ Ⓑ Ⓒ Ⓓ
3	Ⓐ Ⓑ Ⓒ Ⓓ
4	Ⓐ Ⓑ Ⓒ Ⓓ

Part 2

No.	Answer
1	Ⓐ Ⓑ Ⓒ
2	Ⓐ Ⓑ Ⓒ
3	Ⓐ Ⓑ Ⓒ
4	Ⓐ Ⓑ Ⓒ
5	Ⓐ Ⓑ Ⓒ

／9

Unit 2

Part 3

No.	Answer	No.	Answer
1	Ⓐ Ⓑ Ⓒ Ⓓ	11	Ⓐ Ⓑ Ⓒ Ⓓ
2	Ⓐ Ⓑ Ⓒ Ⓓ	12	Ⓐ Ⓑ Ⓒ Ⓓ
3	Ⓐ Ⓑ Ⓒ Ⓓ		
4	Ⓐ Ⓑ Ⓒ Ⓓ		
5	Ⓐ Ⓑ Ⓒ Ⓓ		
6	Ⓐ Ⓑ Ⓒ Ⓓ		
7	Ⓐ Ⓑ Ⓒ Ⓓ		
8	Ⓐ Ⓑ Ⓒ Ⓓ		
9	Ⓐ Ⓑ Ⓒ Ⓓ		
10	Ⓐ Ⓑ Ⓒ Ⓓ		

／12

Unit 3

Part 4

No.	Answer
1	Ⓐ Ⓑ Ⓒ Ⓓ
2	Ⓐ Ⓑ Ⓒ Ⓓ
3	Ⓐ Ⓑ Ⓒ Ⓓ
4	Ⓐ Ⓑ Ⓒ Ⓓ
5	Ⓐ Ⓑ Ⓒ Ⓓ
6	Ⓐ Ⓑ Ⓒ Ⓓ
7	Ⓐ Ⓑ Ⓒ Ⓓ
8	Ⓐ Ⓑ Ⓒ Ⓓ
9	Ⓐ Ⓑ Ⓒ Ⓓ

／9

READING SECTION

Unit 4

Part 5

No.	Answer
1	Ⓐ Ⓑ Ⓒ Ⓓ
2	Ⓐ Ⓑ Ⓒ Ⓓ
3	Ⓐ Ⓑ Ⓒ Ⓓ
4	Ⓐ Ⓑ Ⓒ Ⓓ
5	Ⓐ Ⓑ Ⓒ Ⓓ
6	Ⓐ Ⓑ Ⓒ Ⓓ
7	Ⓐ Ⓑ Ⓒ Ⓓ
8	Ⓐ Ⓑ Ⓒ Ⓓ
9	Ⓐ Ⓑ Ⓒ Ⓓ
10	Ⓐ Ⓑ Ⓒ Ⓓ

／10

Unit 5

Part 6

No.	Answer	No.	Answer
1	Ⓐ Ⓑ Ⓒ Ⓓ	11	Ⓐ Ⓑ Ⓒ Ⓓ
2	Ⓐ Ⓑ Ⓒ Ⓓ	12	Ⓐ Ⓑ Ⓒ Ⓓ
3	Ⓐ Ⓑ Ⓒ Ⓓ		
4	Ⓐ Ⓑ Ⓒ Ⓓ		
5	Ⓐ Ⓑ Ⓒ Ⓓ		
6	Ⓐ Ⓑ Ⓒ Ⓓ		
7	Ⓐ Ⓑ Ⓒ Ⓓ		
8	Ⓐ Ⓑ Ⓒ Ⓓ		
9	Ⓐ Ⓑ Ⓒ Ⓓ		
10	Ⓐ Ⓑ Ⓒ Ⓓ		

／12

Unit 6

Part 7

No.	Answer
1	Ⓐ Ⓑ Ⓒ Ⓓ
2	Ⓐ Ⓑ Ⓒ Ⓓ
3	Ⓐ Ⓑ Ⓒ Ⓓ
4	Ⓐ Ⓑ Ⓒ Ⓓ
5	Ⓐ Ⓑ Ⓒ Ⓓ
6	Ⓐ Ⓑ Ⓒ Ⓓ
7	Ⓐ Ⓑ Ⓒ Ⓓ
8	Ⓐ Ⓑ Ⓒ Ⓓ
9	Ⓐ Ⓑ Ⓒ Ⓓ
10	Ⓐ Ⓑ Ⓒ Ⓓ
11	Ⓐ Ⓑ Ⓒ Ⓓ

／11

Class :　　　　　　　Name :

※コピーしてお使いください。

LISTENING SECTION

Part 1		Part 2		Part 3		Part 4	
No.	Answer	No.	Answer	No.	Answer	No.	Answer
1	Ⓐ Ⓑ Ⓒ Ⓓ	1	Ⓐ Ⓑ Ⓒ	1	Ⓐ Ⓑ Ⓒ Ⓓ	1	Ⓐ Ⓑ Ⓒ Ⓓ
2	Ⓐ Ⓑ Ⓒ Ⓓ	2	Ⓐ Ⓑ Ⓒ	2	Ⓐ Ⓑ Ⓒ Ⓓ	2	Ⓐ Ⓑ Ⓒ Ⓓ
		3	Ⓐ Ⓑ Ⓒ	3	Ⓐ Ⓑ Ⓒ Ⓓ	3	Ⓐ Ⓑ Ⓒ Ⓓ
		4	Ⓐ Ⓑ Ⓒ				

READING SECTION

Part 5		Part 6	
No.	Answer	No.	Answer
1	Ⓐ Ⓑ Ⓒ Ⓓ	1	Ⓐ Ⓑ Ⓒ Ⓓ
2	Ⓐ Ⓑ Ⓒ Ⓓ	2	Ⓐ Ⓑ Ⓒ Ⓓ
3	Ⓐ Ⓑ Ⓒ Ⓓ	3	Ⓐ Ⓑ Ⓒ Ⓓ
		4	Ⓐ Ⓑ Ⓒ Ⓓ

Part 7(Unit 7)		Part 7(Unit 8)		Part 7(Unit 9)		Part 7(Unit 10)	
No.	Answer	No.	Answer	No.	Answer	No.	Answer
1	Ⓐ Ⓑ Ⓒ Ⓓ	1	Ⓐ Ⓑ Ⓒ Ⓓ	1	Ⓐ Ⓑ Ⓒ Ⓓ	1	Ⓐ Ⓑ Ⓒ Ⓓ
2	Ⓐ Ⓑ Ⓒ Ⓓ	2	Ⓐ Ⓑ Ⓒ Ⓓ	2	Ⓐ Ⓑ Ⓒ Ⓓ	2	Ⓐ Ⓑ Ⓒ Ⓓ
		3	Ⓐ Ⓑ Ⓒ Ⓓ	3	Ⓐ Ⓑ Ⓒ Ⓓ	3	Ⓐ Ⓑ Ⓒ Ⓓ
		4	Ⓐ Ⓑ Ⓒ Ⓓ			4	Ⓐ Ⓑ Ⓒ Ⓓ
		5	Ⓐ Ⓑ Ⓒ Ⓓ			5	Ⓐ Ⓑ Ⓒ Ⓓ

Part 7(Unit 11)		Part 7(Unit 12)		Part 7(Unit 13)		Part 7(Unit 14)	
No.	Answer	No.	Answer	No.	Answer	No.	Answer
1	Ⓐ Ⓑ Ⓒ Ⓓ	1	Ⓐ Ⓑ Ⓒ Ⓓ	1	Ⓐ Ⓑ Ⓒ Ⓓ	1	Ⓐ Ⓑ Ⓒ Ⓓ
2	Ⓐ Ⓑ Ⓒ Ⓓ	2	Ⓐ Ⓑ Ⓒ Ⓓ	2	Ⓐ Ⓑ Ⓒ Ⓓ	2	Ⓐ Ⓑ Ⓒ Ⓓ
3	Ⓐ Ⓑ Ⓒ Ⓓ	3	Ⓐ Ⓑ Ⓒ Ⓓ	3	Ⓐ Ⓑ Ⓒ Ⓓ	3	Ⓐ Ⓑ Ⓒ Ⓓ
4	Ⓐ Ⓑ Ⓒ Ⓓ			4	Ⓐ Ⓑ Ⓒ Ⓓ	4	Ⓐ Ⓑ Ⓒ Ⓓ
5	Ⓐ Ⓑ Ⓒ Ⓓ			5	Ⓐ Ⓑ Ⓒ Ⓓ	5	Ⓐ Ⓑ Ⓒ Ⓓ

Unit 7	Unit 8	Unit 9	Unit 10	Unit 11	Unit 12	Unit 13	Unit 14
／21	／24	／22	／24	／24	／22	／24	／24

Class： 　　　　　Name：

TEXT PRODUCTION STAFF

edited by	編集
Minako Hagiwara	萩原 美奈子
Eiichi Tamura	田村 栄一

cover design by	表紙デザイン
Nobuyoshi Fujino	藤野 伸芳

text design by	本文デザイン
Hiroyuki Kinouchi(ALIUS)	木野内宏行(アリウス)

CD PRODUCTION STAFF

narrated by	吹き込み者
Josh Keller (AmE)	ジョシュ・ケラー (アメリカ英語)
Rachel Walzer (AmE)	レイチェル・ワルザー (アメリカ英語)
Nadia Mckechnie (BrE)	ナディア・マケックニー (イギリス英語)
Emma Howard (BrE)	エマ・ハワード (イギリス英語)
Neil Demaere (CnE)	ニール・デマル (カナダ英語)
Brad Holmes (AsE)	ブラッド・ホームズ (オーストラリア英語)
Stuart O (AsE)	スチュアート・オー (オーストラリア英語)

TOP TIPS FOR THE TOEIC® L&R TEST
考えて解くTOEIC® L&R TEST実践演習

2020年1月20日　初版発行
2020年2月15日　第2刷発行

著　　者	Shari J. Berman
	小林 裕子
	早坂 信
発 行 者	佐野 英一郎
発 行 所	株式会社 成 美 堂
	〒101-0052　東京都千代田区神田小川町3-22
	TEL 03-3291-2261　FAX 03-3293-5490
	https://www.seibido.co.jp

印刷・製本　萩原印刷株式会社

ISBN 978-4-7919-7214-2　　　　　　　　　　Printed in Japan